San Luis • Valley
Illustrated

THE SAN LUIS VALLEY

WITH ILLUSTRATIONS

OF ITS

PUBLIC BUILDINGS, SUMMER RESORTS

AND SOME

OF ITS

RESIDENCES, BUSINESS BLOCKS, MANUFACTORIES   •   •   •

AND CITIZENS

(c) 2003 by Adobe Village Press
All rights reserved.

Library of Congress Cataloging-in-Publication Data
Pelton, A.R.
San Luis Valley Illustrated/A. R. Pelton
ISBN: 0-9644056-7-9
Library of Congress Control Number: 2003090474

2003 reprint edition

Published by
Adobe Village Press
1026 S CR 2 E
Monte Vista, CO 81144/USA
adobevp@fone.net
719-852-5225

INTRODUCTION

San Luis Valley Illustrated was originally published 112 years ago as an advertisement to promote immigration into this unique mountain valley. This little book served to lure good industrious families to set up business in the wholesome towns or to farm the fertile land in the San Luis Valley. Those hard-working folks set down deep roots. Many of their ancestors remained. They continue to prosper and produce the best crops to be found anywhere in the world.

As you read this informative book, you'll find that it is a marvelous and well-written source of history of the San Luis Valley. It was felt that a work such as this should be made readily available to all appreciators of western history. With that thought in mind, this little book was happily reproduced.

Ronald E. Kessler
Adobe Village Press
Monte Vista, CO March 1, 2003

INTRODUCTION · ·

San Luis Valley Illustrated is reprinted by public demand, since there is such a limited number of copies of the original. First published 85 years ago, the author had great hopes for the San Luis Valley. This publication is one of the oldest documents promoting the valley and its potential resources.

The reader should pay particular attention to the text and the author's use of words. The illustrations are not as plain in detail, as each had to be re-photoed from the original screening. However, the photos of old buildings, pioneers and old farm machinery should be preserved for generations to come. It is with this in mind that the 188-page volume is reprinted at this time.

Ross B. Campbell
Ye Olde Print Shoppe
Box 838, Alamosa, Colorado 81101

PREFACE ••

IT is with no small amount of gratification that the publisher presents this volume to the public. The object of the work will be at once made manifest to those who peruse its pages. The intention has been to give the SAN LUIS VALLEY a true exposition of its magnificent resources and mercantile and manufacturing advantages, its past growth and future possibilities, and to do this in a manner that will be at once instructive and authentic.

Thanks are due and tendered to those who have so generously aided us, especially to the press of the Valley.

A. R. PELTON.

Salida, Colo., Dec. 1, 1891.

SIERRA BLANCA

ON LINE OF D. & R. G. RAILROAD

THE SAN LUIS VALLEY

THE semi-torrid heat and fatal cyclones of summer, and the semi-frigid cold and equally fatal blizzards of the Eastern States have of late years led many of its people to ask of themselves and their neighbors if there is not some place of residence where these things can be avoided, and where, at the same time, support may be secured for themselves and families, and something laid by for a rainy day and advancing years. The result of these inquiries has been a large emigration to the westward, and lands that but a few years since were looked upon as barren and desert, are now found to be of the most fertile character and productiveness. The far out West, even to the shores of the Pacific ocean, has received a large addition to its population, and the State of Colorado has and is receiving a large increase in this direction, and will continue so to do, as her advantages and resources become more fully known, until, in time, her agricultural and horticultural interests will rank according to the position which their importance shall demand. As a great proportion of the lands of the Eastern and Middle States are rich and productive, it is evident that climate will have much to do in influencing those of that section who desire a change. The writer hereof has lived in different sections of the country for considerable portions of time, including the New England States, Minnesota, Iowa, Kansas, New Mexico, California and Colorado, and hence knows whereof he speaks when asserting that in some particulars the climatic conditions of Colorado are not equaled by those of any other part of the Union, and these are the conditions most conducive to comfortable living and a healthful existence. Owing to its average elevation above sea level—3,000 to 15,000 feet—it is never subject to the muggy, oppressive, debilitating heat of the east and south, nor to the devastating cyclones which carry destruction and death to all in their path. Because of its distance from the ocean it is free from the damp atmosphere and frequent fogs incident to all coast climates, injurious and fatal to many an unsuspecting and ignorant resident there; while the proximity of the ever snow-clad mountains insures cool nights and restful sleep.

Yet though it is true that climate is a very essential ingredient for the comfort and health of man, and while in California it has been sold for hundreds of dollars per acre, it is equally true that climate alone will not support life. This being the case, men will ask what other advantages does a given locality possess in a productive way for the maintenance of health and increase of wealth? For many years the resources of Colorado have been looked upon as almost entirely mineral in character, and "Pike's Peak or Bust" in days gone by meant a search for hidden treasures deep in the bowels of Mother Earth, which sometimes resulted in a competence or a fortune, and sometimes, too, in "Busted, by thunder." Of late years, however, it has been demonstrated that the State of Colorado possess immense agricultural possibilities, and that her valleys and plains have a fertile soil, only needing water to cause them to bud and blossom as the rose, with beauty and productiveness. Having said this much by way of introduction, it is the intention now to speak of the great valleys or parks found in the State, and which in the near future will prove to be a veritable garden for the farmer and horticulturist. Reference is made to the great San Luis Valley, or park, lying in the southern central portion of the State. The description and relation will be no fancy painting, but solid facts, stated in plain language, and verified by personal observation of the writer in the region itself.

In the sweltering days and uneasy nights of mid-summer, one can hardly conceive of a greater luxury than to hie away to a mountainous region, so far heavenward as to be above the reach of the dense miasmas and fogs of the low lands, and the heavy, dull, heated atmosphere of those only a few hundred or a thousand feet above the sea level; to enjoy by day the cool breezes of mid-air which have not been raised to oven heat by the caloric absorbed from the sun-scorched soil; and to sleep at night under blankets where the thermometer seldom stays above 45 or 50 degrees, and never above 60 degrees during ten good hours. For a brief period of mid-day the direct, unobstructed sun's rays are as piercing as at the lower levels, but these are easily warded off by a broad-brimmed hat, or sombrero, or a sun shade of thick fabric. The rarefied air, comparatively free from vapor, does not absorb these rays, and so does not reach a high figure on the thermometer scale, seldom above 80 to 85 degrees in the house or in any shade, in the hottest hours of the day. The ground, cooled at night by the cold airwaves descending from high peaks or ridges, often snow-clad in summer, does not get so warm during the day as to send up hot currents. Then, the freer perspiration in the dryer atmosphere carries away the surplus heat of the body and keeps the skin at a comfortable temperature. Such are the conditions which the writer enjoyed during his trip through the San Luis Valley.

It seems paradoxical that the further one ascends toward the sun, the cooler it should become, yet we all know this to be the fact; we know that everywhere a region of perpetual snow is reached within less than four miles above the sea level. The sun's rays pass directly through pure air without heating it at all. Moisture-laden atmosphere, only found at the sea level and in low altitudes, catches a portion of the rays and is heated by them; but the chief warmth of the air is gained by contact with heated soil. The air thus warmed, expands and rises, but gives out the heat as it ascends and mixes with the vast mass of cooler layers above; so that, could a balloon ascend six or seven miles above the sea level, the occupant would quickly freeze to death. A trip to the moon, or ten miles in that direction, would be fatal to mortals constituted as we are, even with Jules Verne's oxygen-supplying apparatus; our blood would congeal before reaching the first ten-mile station.

When the multitudes who now try to escape from heat in the two hottest months fully understand the philosophy and the facts, the seaside and most other lower resorts will be deserted, and the high mountain regions will be thickly crowded—especially as the engineers have now learned how to carry the easy-riding and luxurious railway carriages over two-mile-high mountain passes, and higher still, with about the same facility as they could formerly be drawn over the level prairies. In our broad mountain regions there are many hundreds of most attractive, elevated valleys, and we do not wonder that the far-seeing, shrewd managers of all our leading east and west railways are pushing their lines and connections out to surmount the Rockies, the Cordilleras, the Wasatch, the Sierra Nevadas, the Cascades, and other high western ranges.

The size of these elevated mountain valleys and parks and plateaus is surprising to those who have not had their attention called to them. All know something of the Yellowstone Park. How many are aware that this so-called "Valley" where we now write, the "San Luis," hemmed in by long mountain ranges, among the highest on the continent, exceeds in extent the State of Massachusetts, if we include the slopes on the surrounding foot-hills, and that it contains an almost level plain, large enough to set the whole State of Connecticut down upon, where it would stand almost a mile and a half above its present elevation! How many conceive of extensive farms, great fields of wheat, oats, barley, etc., just now ready to yield to the harvesters so many bushels per acre of extra grain that even the fertile prairies of the Mississippi Valley and the bottoms of the Red River of the North, would have to yield the palm? But of the agricultural features and capabilities of this Valley we will speak later. Intimately connected with the future of our great country, it is a subject little understood by nine-tenths of the people, farmers or others, east of the Mississippi and the Missouri, or by many living some distance west of these rivers. Yet the subject is of great interest to every American, because, about four-tenths—or nearly one-half of the entire surface of the United States, excluding Alaska—is incapable of profitable cultivation under the natural conditions of rainfall. If one-fourth, or even one-tenth or one-twentieth of this arid half can be made to excel in food and other products the fertile regions of the Mississippi Valley, and more profitably so, it is certainly of great interest to all citizens, to business men, to statesmen, and especially to the surplus agricultural population in the older States, who are seeking for themselves or sons, new fields for labor and enterprise, and desirable homes for themselves and their families. As intimated by a recent writer, the subject of irrigation is interesting, indeed important, to a very large class of cultivators in all the older rain-belt States, even where drainage is one of the leading agricultural improvements. As already intimated, in the moist climate of England and in many places on the continent, irrigation is the source of greatest and most profitable crops, and water, rightly used, is very often the richest fertilizer that can be applied to a field. Of its utility within the natural rain-belt, or east of longitude 98° or 100°—a line running north and south through central Kansas and Nebraska, and in a few limited localities further west and northwest, we must leave for future consideration and explanation. Let us now consider irrigation

as respects the one-third or four-tenths of our country, termed the Arid Regions.

As before mentioned, this valley is in the southern central portion of the State, on the 106th degree of longitude, and between parallels 36° and 38° 30' of latitude, the northern limit being nearly on a parallel with St. Louis, Mo., on the east, and Sacramento, Cala., on the west. The total length of the valley is about 210 miles, of which 150 miles are in the State of Colorado, and its average width from 60 to 80 acres. This gives an area of about 10,000 square miles, or 6,400,000 miles, being longer than the entire State of Connecticut, which is not the smallest State in the Union. This area of land, well cultivated, is capable of supporting a population of hundreds of thousands of people, besides furnishing a large surplus for exportation from the valley, to exchange for such necessaries and luxuries of life as are not raised here.

One might naturally suppose that from the latitude of this region (on a parallel below that of St. Louis, Mo.), that the heat of summer would be oppressive. This is entirely off-set by the elevation of the San Luis Park above

sea level, and its surrounding country. The whole valley is at an altitude of from 6,000 to 8,000 feet above the sea, averaging about 7,000 feet. This secures to the country a comparatively cool climate, when contrasted with some eastern "spells" of weather. Were it not for natural protecting barriers, the winds here might render the valley very uncomfortable for a place of residence. But surrounding it on all sides, except the south, rise vast mountain chains, some peaks of which reach an elevation of nearly 15,000 feet—6,000 to 8,000 feet higher than the floor of the valley. These serve as a protection against fierce winds, and at the same time afford a panorama of surpassing beauty in the variety of grand, picturesque scenery which they present to view, whichever way the eye may be turned. Speaking of the location, extent and elevation of the country, leads very naturally to the climatic conditions found here, which are dependent upon these freaks of nature. For nature has everywhere produced elevations, depressions, configurations of surface, when moved upon by the powerful forces of creative energy, that in their turn are the causes of other

THE SAN LUIS VALLEY

effects seen and experienced in different localities. Referring them to the climate of the San Luis Valley, so far as it has an influence upon the comfort of living, it may, perhaps, be all summed up in one sentence, namely: that taking it the year round, the climate is excelled by that of no other locality in the country, and equaled by very few (if any) other portions, for comfort and health. The seasons of spring, summer, fall and winter are not so plainly marked and divided as in other localities further east, though existing to a certain extent here. Owing to the elevation and consequent rarefaction of the atmosphere, the sun's rays penetrate the intervening air more easily than in a dense atmosphere. And because of the elevation and surrounding mountains, when the sun has disappeared the air cools rapidly. This gives both in summer and winter warm days and cool nights. Were it not for this state of climate crops would mature in summer, and the resting hours of life (night) would not be so peaceful and beneficial to the weary mortal. But while this is true, it is also a fact that extremes of heat or cold are not known here. The thermometer rarely goes

above 85° in summer, nor below 15° under in winter. The average in summer probably is 70° to 80,° and in winter (day time) 20° to 40° above; though there are no statistical figures of value in this connection, the writer making the estimate from his own observations and inquiries on the subject. But in considering these temperatures, it must be remembered that the dryness of the air in this valley (as elsewhere) makes a great difference in the effects of heat and cold upon persons, the difference being from 10° to 20,° so far as it is felt by the individual. That is, one can endure 90° of heat here with more comfort than he can 75° or 80° in an Eastern State. And the same way with cold; 20° below has no more perceptible effect on one than zero cold in Mississippi States.

Then the elevation and dryness of the atmosphere gives to it an elastic, exhilarating, tonic quality never found in sea level air, except it may be right on the ocean beach. One feels "braced up," strengthened and stimulated by inhaling the prevailing breezes, especially in the morning and evening, when it is so cool and refreshing. But while this is the

case the new comer to these altitudes finds that he needs all the breath he can get; for a run of a few rods will leave him panting like a race-horse at the end of a heat. However, this is the only effect of the light air, and the longer one stays in the valley the less he feels it. Of course with such an atmosphere, clear, light, electrical, and the snow-capped mountains all around, there are gorgeous sun-rises and sun-sets, and innumerable scenic effects produced by clouds and sunshine. From clouds come rain and snow, but in this valley there is comparatively little of either. Clouds are continually forming on the mountains, but they soon disappear beneath the rays of the sun or leak out along the mountain tops in rain or snow. In the winter time there are flurries of snow in the valley hardly ever exceeding two or three inches in depth and usually remaining on the ground but a short time. The rainy season is during the months of July and August, when short showers visit the valley nearly every day—sometimes two or three of them in a single day, but lasting only an hour or so at a time. These rains are of some benefit to growing crops, and sprinkle down any loose dust that may have higher aspirations. Altogether, about twelve inches of moisture is precipitated during the year.

But there is no climate that is perfection in all respects, and neither is the climate of the San Luis Valley, and a faithful presentation of facts must include the one that for six or eight weeks of the year, there is rather more coltishness to the airy elements than is either necessary or comfortable. This is from about the middle of April to the middle of June. At this time the valley has got well warmed by the spring and summer sun, while the mountain peaks on all sides are yet covered with snow. The sun rises in the morning and heats the lower air to a considerably higher temperature than that of the snow-clad mountains and so, obeying a law of nature, along about noon each day the cooler air of the elevated regions comes sweeping down into the valley to take the place of the warmer light air which ascends skyward. Sometimes the effect of this is only a gratefully cooling breeze, and at other times it assumes the character of a lively zephyr that reminds one of days upon Kansas and Nebraska prairies. However, these breezes never rise to the dignity of cyclones or hurricanes, or even a respectable prairie wind, and as they last only a few weeks in the year one need take no account of them, compared with other localities. Besides, as the valley becomes settled up and groves are grown on farms as elsewhere in the West, the slight effect of these atmospheric disturbances will be entirely done away with about the houses and barns. As soon as the snow has melted from the mountains, the causes of these winds are gone and they cease. This climate is especially suited to those who are victims to lung troubles, asthma, and the like, and is in fact of great advantage in any ailment where debility is a characteristic. The dry air has tonic, stimulating and electrical qualities that give new tone and elasticity to the weakened constitution, and life and vigor to the system by its preventative and curative properties.

This being a region where nearly all agriculture must be carried on by irrigation, and where the rays of the sun have much to do with the growth and maturity of crops, the lay of the land is a question of much importance to an intending settler. There are localities where irrigation is necessary and water is plenty, but the surface of the land is so uneven that it is almost impossible to use the precious fluid for crop producing purposes. Again, there are fertile lands at high elevations, but the slope of the surface is such that it does not receive the full benefit of the sun's warm rays, and the soil is cold and unfruitful. In the San Luis Valley, however, nature seems to have planned almost perfectly in these respects, for the benefit of coming generations. The general slope of the land is gently toward the centre, and at the same time southward for two hundred miles. And yet so gradual is this gradation, that one can scarcely tell from a given point which way the descent is. In the northern end of the valley on the eastern side, the water shed is toward the San Luis and Saguache creeks, which flow southerly along the west centre, and lose their waters in a group of lakes near the base of a high mountain. These waters, called the San Luis Lakes, are fresh with no visible outlet, the loose soil absorbing all overplus of moisture. Some sixteen or eighteen small streams from the mountains find their way into these creeks and lakes at various points, and considerable areas of natural grass lands and numerous trees are found along their banks.

Nearly opposite and directly west of these lakes a large stream of water debouches from a mountain pass and goes rushing away down the valley—faster and faster carrying volumes of *aqua pura*, till it finally loses itself in the briny waters of the Gulf of Mexico. This is the famous river, Rio Grande Del Norte—the Grand River of the North. As the arteries of the body are the life of man, so is this great river the life of this vast valley. Its precious fluid will prove the agency that will cause this region ere long to be one of the garden spots of the world. This stream carries an immense volume of water along its course through this region, constantly and everlastingly fed by melting snow fields of the higher altitudes. To exemplify the fine lay of the land for irrigation purposes here, it is only necessary to call attention to the use made of the water of the river near the point where it issues from the mountains. At this place an immense canal taps the river and flows off to the north along the foothills, carrying 1,620,000,000 gallons of water every twenty-four hours when open to its full capacity, a distance of some fifty miles,

emptying its residue into the Saguache creek which flows southward on the east side of the valley. Just below where this canal is taken out another ditch of about one-half this capacity taps the river on the south side and flows off southward for a distance of some forty-five miles. Each of these ditches is a young river in itself, and is capable of irrigating a vast acreage of land. The general southern slope of the valley gives the sun's rays full opportunity to get in their work on the growing vegetation, which is done with bountiful effect, as noted further on. Coming down to smaller areas, it may be said that as a rule the land surface is excellently fitted for the appropriation of water for irrigation purposes. There are, of course, plains here and there, where there is some roughness—but generally speaking the land could not lie better for the distribution of water over its surface.

What is irrigation? It may be said that in the most powerful nations of the past, Babylonia, Persia, Egypt, a large part of the Roman and Grecian Empires, and now in most of India (Hindostan, with a sixth of the population of the globe), in a considerable part of Italy, in

much of France and Spain, the chiefest and best productions of the soil are obtained mainly through irrigation. Perhaps it is not an over estimate to say that without irrigation, one-fourth of the population of the earth would be without sufficient food to sustain life. We have just had the privilege of looking over an extensive private library containing scores of different books, including numerous large octavo volumes, all upon this single subject of irrigation.

Irrigation in the present use of the term means the artificial application of water to the soil, by several methods. There is the "main canal" or ditch which brings water taken from streams that may be a mile or two, or scores of miles away. A "lateral" comes out of one side and extends several rods, or even miles, to the upper side of a field, into a plow-furrow nearly on a level, and the water in this case spreads out each way. From this head furrow very small ones are made with a hoe, or quicker with a small single-horse plow. They are run in such direction, required by the lay of the land, as will give them only a slight descent. A hoe or shovel full of earth into the plow furrow at each entrance of these little ditches keeps them closed. When the land needs water, the little "gate," or sliding-board at the canal, is raised as far as needed to let in the required amount of water. This is raised or lowered from time to time, as seen to be necessary. The large plow furrow being filled with water, the irrigator opens or closes the upper ends of the small furrows by taking out a shovel or hoefull of earth. The operator walks over the field, and where water enough is not flowing out in any place he, with a shovel or hoe, clips off a bit of earth from the side of the small ditch or furrow, or stops the flow at any point by throwing in a trifle of soil. In this way he can, in an hour or two, give an entire field what would be equal to a heavy soaking rain. This may be done so deeply down, one or even two feet, that the growing crop may flourish through the hottest season or drouth, without irrigating again.

Where water goes deep down, it is only very slowly evaporated from the surface, while the roots of the crop grow downward so far as to find a good deal of natural moisture in the soil. Usually only two or at most three such irrigations are needed on a wheat crop, grown on a soil which is literally a dry ash heap. The number of irrigations and the amount of water at each flowing depends a good deal upon the character of the subsoil. Some land requires only a single flowing, along in May or June. Sometimes a flooding about the heading-out time will produce very heavy grain kernels. Sometimes the ground is well flooded before the seed is sown and once or twice afterward, unless there is an unusual fall of rain. Most farmers using irrigation, rather prefer *no* rain. Having a supply of water in the canal to use whenever needed, they prefer continual hot sunshine, which pushes growth forward most rapidly.

In most of the irrigable, arid regions, these canals are taken out high up a river or stream which is fed by the melting of snows on the mountain tops in May, June and July, just the time when plenty of water in the canal is most needed. The canals are carried along with a descent of only 1½ to 2 feet per mile, winding around hills or uneven ground to maintain a uniform grade. If the ground and the stream descend rapidly the canal may thus be carried scores of miles, and at its end be 20, 50, 100 or more feet above the parent stream. The side canals are taken out at different places and similary carried over or around uneven land, so that a single main canal may irrigate tens or hundreds of thousands of acres. For example, a canal from a stream in the Rocky Mountains, by following the sides of knolls, valleys and hills, may take water hundreds of miles to supply the parched farms in Eastern Colorado.

The above is an ordinary method on grain and grass fields, which may be flooded all over deeply or thinly. The flooding may be continued during a whole day, or more, if desired. For corn, potatoes and other crops *in rows*, for fruit trees, etc., one method is to have the rows run *with* the downward incline of the surface; then run one furrow along the upper side of the field, to receive the water. A small opening with a hoe against the furrows or hollows between the rows, or opened every second or third or fourth one, allows the water to flow along the furrows and soak into each side of them as long and deeply as desired. The main lateral ditch is usually a permanent one, made by a few plow furrows, not so deep as to prevent easy driving over it. The small field channels are usually obliterated in the general plowing, new ones being made or left in the form and in the places where needed when the crop is put in. A wheat or other grain or grass field is often flooded over its whole surface by openings as needed from the ditch along the higher side. Another method, where land is very valuable, and permanent improvements are desirable, is to run perforated pipe, like drain pipe, 1½ to 3 feet underground, and let water into the heads of them, to soak *up* into the soil. In this way one has a positive and permanent moisture in the soil.

On a vast number of farms all over the country in the rain belt, clear to the Atlantic, the fields are seldom level, though nearly so. It is very often practicable to run a furrow across the higher end or side of the field, and have a supply of water to flood the grass or grain, or run down between crops in rows, so as to resist any destructive drouth; and often doubling the crops, even in an ordinary dry season.

The water supply may come from a stream, or from a reservoir at the outlets of underdrains on still higher ground. A hollow place, natural or artificial, at some point where the surface is higher than the irrigable places, may be kept full of water from an artesian well, or very easily from a windmill over a well. There are tens of thousands of farms in all the settled States —hundreds of thousands in the aggregate —where such simple provision would, one year with another, increase the actual crops enough to pay 10, 20 or 50 per cent. on the cost of the fixtures required. As before stated, the most perfect system of farming is to arrange so as to carry off surplus moisture in early spring or after extraordinary rain storms, or in a very wet season, and then to have means ready to supply needed moisture when the heavens withhold it. Such a farm averages double the crop of one not thus provided, other things being equal, and with the same cost for working, seedings, etc.

From the above it will be seen that a farm needs to vary from a level not more than a few inches in a hundred feet, to allow a very good system of irrigation.

Irrigation farming is the most desirable. This statement will seem singularly inexact, if not foolish, to very many of our readers. It will even be jeered at by the great mass of people between the Atlantic and the Mississippi, simply and only because they do not understand it. We speak from a good deal of examination of the subject. "Seeing is believing," if the seeing is intelligent and unbiased, and especially if against one's preconceived notions or opinions. The farmer who has a soil containing an abundance of all the needed elements, in a proper state of fineness, can not but deem himself happy if he has always ready at hand the means of rapidly and cheaply supplying all the water needed by his soil and growing crops, just when and in just such quantities as are needed. Happier still may he be if, besides fearing no drouth, he has no rainfall to interrupt his labors, or to injure his growing or harvested crops. And happier still may he be when he knows that he need have few if any "off years," and knows that the water he admits to his fields, at will, is freighted with rich fertilizing elements, usually far more valuable to the growing crop than any he can purchase and apply at a costly rate—a cost that makes serious inroads upon the profits of a majority of farmers cultivating the worn-out or deteriorated soils in the older states, year by year. Fertilizers are already often needed for the most profitable culture on many farms in Iowa, Minnesota, Eastern Kansas, and Nebraska, in Missouri, and in all States east of those named.

The above are no imaginative statements, but are based upon actual observations—upon a study of the soils, their conditions and wants,—so much so that we unhesitatingly assert that if allowed to-day to make a choice of a farm for our own future tillage, among the best in the rain-fall States or among the best of those only cultivable by irrigation, we should certainly choose the latter. This is with the understanding that railways have now made such regions readily accessible to markets—markets, as yet, better than those in the East; and that there is already so large a class of intelligent, moral people settled in these regions and fast coming into them, as to make society as desirable as in the older States.

Besides what is stated above, let us consider these points: First.—All soils are formed from comminuted rocks, with a little addition of organic matter. Second.—Crops,—all plants and trees— get most of their materials for growth from the air through the leaves. (We need not here discuss the theory as to the derivation of some of the nitrogen or other gases through the sap). Third.—A ton of earth carefully weighed and yielding a ton of clover or other crop, will weigh

more after the cropping than before, even though so covered that only pure water is admitted. Fourth.—All crops and plants need a soil in such a condition that roots can penetrate it. These roots act as braces to hold the upright stems, bearing leaves, which through their myriads of mouths absorb food from the air. The roots also take up from the soil the moisture, which as sap, circulates through the stems, receiving the food gathered by the leaves, carries and deposits it where needed for growth or repairs, just as our blood carries the dissolved food particles and deposits them all over the body where needed for growth or repair, or for producing warmth. But as crops used for food need some phosphates, iron, etc., to build up the frame-work (bones) and for other purposes, the sap must collect these needed mineral elements from the soil. Fifth.— Two most important mineral constituents, the phosphates and potash, are very poorly supplied in most old soils. They have been carried off in removed crops, in meat carcasses and dairy products grown from the soil; and they have been washed out of those lands subject to drenching rains.

The miner asks as to the rocks, their

character, trend, dips, and angles. The lumberman asks about the timber its rise, "get-at-ability," cleavage and quality. But to the farmer, the character of the soil and what it will produce in kind, quality and quantity, are important points, when desiring to locate a home. The soil of the Valley has been formed from volcanic productions, ground to powder by the action of ice and water, in by-gone ages. The mountains on all sides give evidence of their volcanic formation, and here and there, all over the Valley may be picked up lava stones of various sizes from a pinhead to a boulder. Along the foothills the soil is rather coarse and gravelly, becoming finer towards the center of the Valley. Along the river and creek bottoms there is more or less sand, the same as in all other localities. It is a well known fact that this volcanic soil is of the richest character known for crop and fruit bearing, the records of southern France, Italy, and Spain bearing witness to this fact, in their bounteous crops and fruits.

The land is light and porous, the streams in many cases losing their waters in its depths before reaching any other creek or lake. It can be ploughed and a crop put in at any seasonable time, after removing the vegetation growing upon it. The Eastern emigrant who reaches this place expecting to see a vast plain covered with green grass and blooming flowers will find himself badly left on that deal. On the river and creek bottoms and in places along the foothills, the grasses do grow naturally and luxuriantly, furnishing nutritious food for stock the year round. But on the plains or prairies there is no grass to speak of, and the natural production is grease wood and chico—a kind of evergreen shrub growing from a few inches to three or four feet in height. This growth is gotten rid of, usually, with comparative ease in preparing for crops. Three railroad rails are bound together, a team hitched to each end and the irons then dragged over the surface, breaking off the growth, in the same way that the Western farmer breaks corn stalks in winter. This work should also be done in winter, when the stuff is frozen and brittle, and several acres per day can be cleared in this way, leaving the land ready for ploughing and cropping, after burning up the overgrowth. When the ground is seeded and the water properly applied the result is sure and

abundant crops of grain and vegetables. And right here is the beauty of irrigation farming. No fear of wet or dry weather. The farmer don't care for the weather, be it one way or the other. He has in his own control all elements of growth, and though it may be somewhat more of trouble than a natural rainfall, yet he is always sure of returns if he knows his own business and attends to it properly.

The questions as to what crops are grown and what may be grown, and how abundantly, require separate answers.

Wheat, oats, barley, peas, potatoes, in fact all kinds of small grains and vegetables have been and are raised, and with proper attendance and culture yield large returns. Grasses grown by irrigation are a luxuriant crop here, alfalfa yielding from six to eight tons per acre per year, and timothy and red-top producing large quantities also. But as in all farming countries, so it may be and will be here. There are good farmers and poor ones; lazy men and industrious men, and as in justice, industry and care receive the best rewards from Mother Earth. A good average yield of grains in an ordinary sized farm is, wheat, 25 to 30 bushels; oats, 35 to 45 bushels; barley, 40 to 50

bushels; potatoes, 250 to 400 bushels. Of course some examples are known where a field of wheat has yielded 50 bushels; oats, 80 bushels; barley, 60 bushels; potatoes, 500 bushels, but these are not average crops from year to year. Yet it should be the ambition of every farmer to reach the highest possibilities with the soil and water under his control. Such vegetables as turnips, beets, cabbages, and onions seem to have found in the San Luis Valley their natural home, and yield enormous crops of perfect quality and size.

As for fruits, it is well known that all kinds of berries, strawberries, raspberries, blackberries, currants, gooseberries, etc., etc., raise bountiful crops of delicious flavor, when given water and care. Thus will be seen that soil and climate are equal to the production of a varied and bountiful supply of the necessities and luxuries wanted for comfortable homes. True, in some spots over this vast area of country there is something of an excess of mineral salts in the land. A large surplus of the alkalies is necessary for the growing of grains and in many places it has to be supplied artificially, but an excess of it is also injurious to the producing qualities of the soil. In this Valley, however, there is very little such land and even where it does exist in small spots, continued irrigation will remove it in two or three years. In this connection it may be appropriate to pass a few remarks upon farming by irrigation.

It may not be necessary to say that irrigation consists in conducting the water of streams and reservoirs upon the land by means of canals and ditches for the purpose of furnishing necessary moisture to growing crops or seed in the ground. This is known to all and it is also a fact that it is the surest way of farming. It is the only method of agriculture that can be pursued in most of the San Luis Valley. But let not the "rainy" farmer who goes to an irrigating country think that he "knows it all," else he may come to know his ignorance by dear experience. Irrigation is a simple process and easily learned, but it must be learned to a certain extent to insure success. It has been in use for thousands of years, but there is something of it yet to be learned by almost any person. It requires a knowledge of the soil, the climate, and the crop to be irrigated. Some lands require a little water and often. Other lands require much water at long intervals. It is the same way with crops. One kind requires more, another less water. For little water may dry out the grain and much may prevent it from ripening. A large amount of water may give large size to fruit, while less gives better flavor. The number of times that crops need irrigating in this Valley varies from one to four times during the season, according to crop and soil. But the average is about three times, and one man can care for from 60 to 80 acres during a year. The manner in which water should be handled and applied can be easily learned by inquiries from those who have lived in a given locality, and know something of irrigating, and also by observations.

From earliest known times in San Luis Park, this Valley has been the stockman's paradise. The summers are cool and the winters are mild; the grass growing in the river and creek bottoms and among the foothills furnishes cured hay, standing, for winter feed, and in summer the mountains afford fine range for all kinds of stock, so that animals thrive the year round without being hand-fed, and furnish the best quality of beef and mutton for all markets. Before the irrigating canals were proposed the whole country was a pastoral region. More than 300 years ago the Mexicans occupied the land with their herds, and it has been continuously occupied in like manner by them, and by Americans ever since. There are now many large herds owned in the Valley and a number of fine stock ranches where blooded animals—cattle, horses and sheep —are bred with the most successful results. The plentitude of feed, water and climate make it one of the finest stock regions in the country. This is not an exaggeration, but a solid fact. It is one of the great beauties of the San Luis Valley that while the climate and soil are of the best, and the lay of the land is so favorable to irrigating purposes, there is an abundance of the finest water that can be found on the continent. The mountains round about are loaded with millions of tons of frozen snow during the winter season, and this melting in the spring and summer furnishes an abundance of pure, soft water, which flows down over the surface in numerous creeks, and underneath, in great volumes. The Rio Grande carries a great amount of water, and by sinking wells from 10 to 15 feet in almost any part of the Valley a bountiful supply is secured. As if this was not more than enough, artesian flowing wells may be secured at depths varying from 80 to 250 feet, which will furnish several hundreds (or, perhaps, thousands,) of barrels of cold, soft water per day for domestic and irrigating purpose. It would seem that the supplies of water in these ways could not be excelled by any device of nature. The whole Valley seems to have water under it, as these artesian wells have been found at distances 40 and 50 miles apart, in different sections of the country. Water is conducted over a large portion of the valley by huge canals from the river, some owned by corporations and some by private parties.

The supply of fuel in and around the valley is fully adequate to any demand that is or may be made. There is a small amount of timber on the rivers and creeks, while the mountains all around from five to twenty miles are covered with forests of pine and spruce, some of the trees being of large size. Coal is also found in the mountains, though no working mines of it are yet opened on the valley sides. What coal is used is shipped in from mines near by, and sells at $5 to $7 per ton. Cedar posts and lumber for building may be obtained in any quantities in the mountains, posts costing eight to ten cents each and lumber $12 and $14 per thousand feet at the mountain mills, or $18 and $20 in the towns. There are coal beds within a few miles of the valley undeveloped, and about seventy miles to the southwest are large areas of coal and oil lands, which will furnish large quantities of these products for home consumption at low prices. While reference has heretofore been made almost exclusively to the agricultural resources of the San Luis, it must not be forgotten that all through the mountains encircling this great basin, there are treasures of unknown valuable minerals. Gold, silver, lead, copper and iron are found, and several mines of these are opening up, affording a home market for many products, and also increasing the productive capacity of the country. One iron mine in the north end of the Valley ships large quantities of ore to the iron and steel works at Pueblo, and the country has been but little prospected as yet. As before remarked, these industries furnish a home market for agricultural products, and large quantities are also shipped out by rail even in the present undeveloped state of the country. Colorado sends out of the State nearly $4,000,000 annually for farm products, every one of which can be raised in this Valley. It is safe to say that no other section of the country presents such advantages in the way of climate, soil, abundance of fuel, timber and water, as does this valley to those who are willing to go to a new country and pursue farming by irrigation, or such other branches of industry as the development of this section may warrant. The country is comparatively a new one, giving all an equal chance. There are some old settlers who have been in the Valley from eight to fourteen years, but the great majority, especially in the country, are only residents for four, three or two years, or even less. Lands are still cheap. The canal companies who own lands here will sell land on long time and favorable terms, at from $3 to $10 per acre, and will furnish water at from 50 cents to $1.00 per acre, for irrigation; or will sell land and a perpetual water right to free water, for from $7 to $20 per acre. Government lands for pre-emption, homestead, and timber claims may still be had in some localities, and ''relinquishments'' in advantageous places may be secured at from $100 to $500 for 160 acres. These "relinquishments" are where men have entered upon the land intending to make homes, have usually made some improvements, and then have become sick of it or want to speculate (as is the case in all new countries), and so want to sell their rights and improvements. There are now some very fine ranches in different parts of the Valley devoted to grain for dairy purposes, the country being also splendidly suited to stock raising, which show what grit, enterprise and a little money can accomplish, and there is still room for thousands more of the same kind, for those who desire to make the necessary efforts to secure them in this much favored section of Uncle Sam's dominions.

Now that we have given a general sketch of the Valley from an agricultural standpoint, let us say a few words relative to it from the manufacturer's and hunter's view. First, then, it should be borne in mind that this particularly favored portion of the great State of Colorado is new—is yet an infant, so to speak; but it is certain to become an exceedingly lusty one. There is abundant material and unlimited opportunities for the establishment of successful manufacturing enterprises of various kinds, among which may be mentioned a smelter, an oat mill, a shirt factory, a potato starch factory, a soap factory, a wagon factory, a canning establishment, a tannery, an oil mill, a paper mill, a woolen mill, an agricultural implement factory, a creamery and a marble manufactory. Any of the above manufacturing establishments will be suitably encouraged and are sure to reward their promoters.

The lover of sport will find in proper season in the San Luis Valley splendid shooting. Wild ducks make the San Luis lakes their headquarters in flocks of thousands; there are still quite a number of deer and antelope in the woods, while grouse, sage hens, rabbits and small game are to be found in great abundance.

SAGUACHE COUNTY

THE methods of advertising heretofore adopted by many of the syndicates and companies who have been trying to stimulate immigration to and investment in Colorado lands, have in many instances proven a detriment instead of an advantage to the best interests of the State, for the simple reason that gross exaggeration and falsehood have been leading features in many of these advertisements. True, a great many people have come to Colorado and the West upon the representations made in these high sounding advertisements, who, upon their arrival, would as a matter of course, see that they had been deceived by false representations and would leave the State in disgust, and advise their friends to remain away, thus checking rather than encouraging development, which has, nothwithstanding these baneful influences, been marvelous, because the true merit of Colorado has not and can not be destroyed by the falsehood of boomers and speculators. The foregoing facts we consider necessary before proceeding to give a brief sketch descriptive of the resources and outlook, present and future, of Saguache County, which contains about 3,500 square miles of land, about 1,000 square miles, or about 640,-000 acres of which are located in the north end of the great San Luis Valley, the remainder and larger portion of the county lying in the foothills and mountains to the north and west; the famous Sangre de Christo range forming the eastern boundary. At least 80 to 90 per cent of the valley land in the county is perfectly level, with a rich soil, made very productive when brought under cultivation and irrigation. About 50 per cent of this Valley land is yet vacant and open to settlement, there being also large tracts of State and school lands that may be bought cheap or leased on easy terms.

Irrigation is absolutely necessary in this Valley to the production of good crops of any kind, and with irrigation and proper cultivation a failure is impossible, climatic and other conditions being favorable; and this matter of irrigation, a source of much trouble and annoyance in some parts of the mountain country, has been practically solved and settled in Saguache County. About three years ago the first flow of artesian water was obtained in this county at a depth of 150 feet. Other wells were sunk during the following season and good strong flows of water were secured that only grow stronger as time passes, proving beyond the possibility of a doubt that these artesian wells, of which there are over 400 in the county, will afford a never-failing supply of water, together with large canals running from the Rio Grande River on the south through the Valley lands of the county, and the Saguache River and other mountain streams conveying water into the Valley afford an ample supply of water for irrigation and domestic use. The average depth of these artesian wells is about 150 feet, the average cost not exceeding $100.

There is little timber in the Valley, but the surrounding foothills and mountains (all vacant grazing land) are covered with pine, spruce and cedar timber, from which a never-failing supply of fuel fence posts, lumber and building material can always be obtained. Wild game is plentiful in the mountains and the streams are well stocked with trout; the water in the mountain streams and springs is healthful; the air is dry, light and invigorating; the climate unequaled—no sudden changes of temperature—making the county a most desirable resort for health seekers and tourists during the summer months.

Parties wishing to visit this county from the East will come from either Denver or Pueblo over the Denver and Rio Grande Railroad via Salida to Villa Grove or Moffat, on the main line of the Denver and Rio Grande, south to Alamosa and thence west to Durango and the southwest.

The Pueblo, Gunnison & Pacific, a broad guage railroad, will, without doubt, be built east and west through the county via Saguache over the Cochetopa pass, which will, when completed, afford ample shipping facilities for the Valley to the mining camps to the west and north and to the centres of trade via the east.

Chamberlin Springs is the nearest railroad point, fourteen miles east.

Sargent, Carnero and Ford Creek are mining camps in the county that must soon come into prominence as producers of gold and silver, which, with the various other mining camps in the county, will give the farmers a good home market for their farm products.

Wheat, oats, rye and barley grow to perfection in this county, the average yield of oats per acre being 50 bushels; wheat, rye and barley averaging about 25 bushels per acre, the quality of the grain being unequaled on the continent.

Potatoes, cabbage, beans, peas and all other vegetables are raised in abundance, and of the very best quality.

Groceries, provisions and all kinds of supplies can be bought nearly as cheap here as elsewhere in the country, so that heads of families who are desirous of coming west to secure homes, if they can bring with them a small amount of money, say $500, need not hesitate to come along, and come soon, before all the choice land is taken and settled upon.

The population of this county is now about 5,000 and before the close of another year it will, no doubt, be increased to three or perhaps five times that number; so come early and secure first choice of land. It is not claimed that this county is a paradise for the stockman, the farmer or invalid. It is not claimed that fortunes can be made here in a day, or a month or at all, without economical management and work; but it is claimed that if a man with small capital desires to engage in stock-raising, good opportunities are here offered for investment and fair profits may be realized from small herds of high grade stock, and we do claim that farming pays here if properly managed; work and good management being required here as elsewhere to insure success. It is also claimed that if you are in poor health and a change of climate is desired, you may come to this county during the summer months with positive assurance of permanent benefits. As a sanitarium, Saguache County has few equals and no superiors in the State.

The O'Neil Hot Springs, one mile north of Saguache, have lately been fitted with commodious bath houses for the accommodation of the public. Some remarkable cures attest to the superior medicinal properties of the water of these springs.

Valley View Hot Springs, on the east side of the county, are becoming famous as a health resort. A good hotel and a number of neat cottages have been erected and are now open for the accommodation of tourists and invalids.

The celebrated Chamberlin Hot Springs, fourteen miles east of Saguache, on the new line of the Denver and Rio Grande Railroad, will be improved and fitted up next season and must surely become a popular resort. Here will be the junction of the southern and western lines of the Denver and Rio Grande road.

Last, but by no means least, Shaw's Hot Mineral Springs, twenty-five miles south of Saguache, are worthy of special mention as a place where the afflicted may go and find relief, the springs having been fitted up with a first-class hotel and the best of accommodations.

No attempt has been made at word painting, but homely truths have been given in a homely way, trusting that no one will be misled thereby.

VILLA GROVE

AMONG the rising towns in the State of Colorado is Villa Grove, situated in Saguache County, on the main line of the Durango division of the Denver and Rio Grande Railroad, midway between Salida and Alamosa, at the golden gate of the famous San Luis Valley.

Located at the foot of Poncha Pass, at an elevation of about 8,000 feet, surrounded on the east by the Sangre de Christo range and on the west by the Cochetopa hills, noted for their ever changing and beautiful mountain scenery, it is endowed with all the charms of nature's loveliness and beauty.

In addition to this the pure and dry atmosphere of the high altitudes makes it both a health and pleasure resort, and one of the most attractive townsites in the State.

About six miles south of Villa Grove are situated the San Luis Hot Springs, and about eight miles from town, one mile south of Orient, are the Fairview Hot Springs, where there are good bathing houses and cottages for invalids who desire to take advantage of these magnetic springs. The springs offer a great relief to all who are afflicted with symptoms of rheumatism, asthma and consumption, and often prove a sure cure.

Villa Grove is particularly favored with a peculiar combination of wonderful natural resources that but few towns in the west possess.

The mountain ranges which surround her are laden with precious metals and unlimited deposits of gold, silver, iron, lead, and copper, lie at her very door.

At Orient, a few miles from town, the

BIRD'S-EYE VIEW OF VILLA GROVE

Colorado Coal and Iron Company have extensive iron mines in operation. About one hundred men are employed there throughout the year, and from one hundred to two hundred tons of iron ore are daily shipped to the smelters in Pueblo and Durango. Bonanza, about sixteen miles distant, shipped about two hundred carloads of ore this season — 1891.

Kerber Creek and San Luis Creek, which traverse the Valley, are lined all along with well improved farms, hay and stock ranches. There is also plenty of merchantable timber in close proximity, and a large saw mill is in operation in Steele Canon. The mountains are also dotted with numerous tie camps, and millions of railroad ties are annually furnished to the Denver and Rio Grande Railroad Company.

Within a short distance from town there are also immense coal fields now in progress of development.

All of these resources, though yet in this embryotic state of development, are a permanent source of support to Villa Grove, and will, in the event of time, bring Villa Grove to the front and make her one of the leading commercial centers of the San Luis Valley. The Denver and Rio Grande Railroad is now sinking a deep artesian well. A depth of three hundred feet has been reached. The prospects for an artesian flow are flattering.

S. E. VAN NOORDEN
Editor and Lawyer

There is room in Villa Grove for a banking and mercantile establishments of all kinds, as well as other minor business branches. It offers an excellent opportunity for the safe and profitable investment of capital and labor.

S. E. VAN NOORDEN.—Mr. Van Noorden came to Colorado in the spring of 1889, and landed at Monte Vista on the twenty-seventh day of May of that year. Being desirous of acquainting himself with the characteristics, advantages and condition of the San Luis Valley, he traveled for three consecutive months across the plains, valleys and mountains, visited the ranches and the mining camps, and furnished a series of valuable articles, the results of his observations, for the Monte Vista *Sun*, which were read with great interest, and won for him a favorable reputation as a writer. Having concluded to locate in the Valley, he embarked in the newspaper business. For some time he published the *San Luis Valley Farmer*. He came to Villa Grove in the spring of 1890, where he has resided ever since, and where he is now engaged in the practice of law and also publishes the *Headlight*, a bright and lively newspaper which has done much good for the town. At the beginning of this year he was appointed County Attorney by the Board of County Commission-

FRANCIS M. HILLS
Chairman Board of County Commissioners,
Saguache County

the general merchandise line, the new firm of Whiteman & Hawkins ranks as leaders. They carry almost everything in the line of general merchandise and country produce. The firm is composed of Mr. D. J. Whiteman and Mr. D. K. Hawkins, both of whom have resided in Villa Grove over five years. They are gentlemen of business ability of a high order and well deserve the esteem in which they are held throughout the Valley.

GEO. W. NORRIS.—The consumption of spirituous liquors, both in the mechanical arts and for medical purposes, is widespread, and of mercantile importance. The question which is of paramount importance in this connection is where to get the purest grade of goods at honest prices. The class of goods which is handled by this gentle-

ers of Saguache County, which office he has so far filled with satisfaction and credit to himself.

WHITEMAN & HAWKINS.—The rapid strides that the Valley has made have caused men of energy and capital to enter into competition in the mercantile arena. Especially is this noticable in Villa Grove, of which in

WHITEMAN & HAWKINS' SUPPLY STORE

LEE C. EAGLES

and unswerving fidelity to the cause of Villa Grove and the San Luis Valley.

THE SAN LUIS HOTEL.—Mr. G. W. Redmond is the whole-souled proprietor of the San Luis Hotel, at Villa Grove, one of the leading hostelries in the Valley and the only first-class house in the town. Prior to locating in this city he lived in Saguache, where he was engaged in the hotel and livery business for about nine years. He has earned a splendid reputation as a hotel man. Mr. Redmond takes great pride in keeping his house up to the highest standard of excellence. The table is always bountifully supplied with the best in the market. The beds are neat and clean, and the rooms tastefully furnished and decorated. The San Luis Hotel is also headquarters for the Villa Grove and

SAN LUIS HOTEL
G. W. Redmond, Proprietor

man represents the product of the most celebrated vintages of both home and foreign countries. Not alone does this apply to liquors, but likewise to cigars, of which he carries a most complete line. Mr. Norris' trade is built upon the enduring basis of mercantile integrity and probity, coupled with the fact that he enjoys a splendid reputation for honesty

A. HENRY SCHWACKENBERG
Justice of the Peace

FRANCIS M. HILLS.—Francis M. Hills, Chairman of the Board of County Commissioners of Saguache County, is now serving his third term. Mr. Hills came to this State from California in November, 1873, locating in Villa Grove in 1879; has five hundred acres immediately adjoining the town of Villa Grove, part of which he used in platting the townsite. He raises all kinds of small fruits and cereals; is fifty-three years old, and is held in the highest esteem by all who know him.

A. HENRY SCHWACKENBERG. — The gentleman whose name heads this sketch is one of the best known and most favorably regarded citizens of the entire San Luis Valley. To hold an office for four consecutive terms is an honor few men attain, and it demonstrates beyond

Saguache stage line. Taking it all in all, there is no better house in the Valley.

LEE C. EAGLES.— Lee C. Eagles is one of the original settlers of the town, and was the first man to say that Villa Grove would make a town, and he is the first man to say that she will become a city—and that within ten years. He discovered petroleum in 1881.

GEO. W. NORRIS'S SALOON

doubt that in order to be thus the object of the confidence of an entire community, it is necessary for a man to be in every manner qualified. Such a man, and such a record has Mr. A. Henry Schwackenberg, who has been Justice of the Peace at Villa Grove during the past four years, and for fair-mindedness, honesty and impartiality, he bears a reputation second to none. Mr. Schwackenberg is also engaged in the boot and shoe, saddlery and harness business, and has been an active member of the business community of Villa Grove for eight years.

MOFFAT

THE new town of Moffat, on the Denver and Rio Grande Railroad, at the north end of the Valley, was laid out by the San Luis Town and Improvement Company during the construction of the new line of road, and its prospects for the future are bright. Its promoters comprise a very strong incorporated body with a capital of $100,000, consisting of prominent men of the State, among them the noted thoroughbred stock raiser, George H. Adams, of Baca Grant No. 4, who is its president; S. N. Wood, retired Cashier of the First National Bank of Denver; Hon. Otto Mears, J. W. Gilluly, Treasurer of the Denver and Rio Grande Railroad, and several other of the road's officials who will seek to make it the best town in Saguache County, of which it is the center. The railroad and town company have expended over $50,000 in improvements, among them a $10,000 hotel, a depot, the best between Salida and Durango, extensive sidetracks and stock yards and a number of artesian wells, including one at a depth of 1,047 feet, one of the best in the State, which is said to afford the best and purest water on the Denver and Rio Grande Railroad.

Owing to its location, Moffat is one of the best shipping points in the Valley, and owing to its wide tributaries it affords a good opening for any branch of business. Its business enterprises are few in number, but they are all first-class. The San Luis Supply Company, incorporated, with John MacLachlan as President, and H. N. Otis, Secretary, is one of the leading mercantile establishments of Southern Colorado, and the drug house of J. W. Rambo & Co. would do honor to a much larger town. The large brick livery stable operated by George H. Adams is first-class in every respect, and is equipped to meet all the demands of the traveling public, and has a large business carrying passengers who leave the cars at Moffat for Saguache and other inland points.

The town supports one of the best weekly papers in Southern Colorado, the *Moffat Ledger*, owned and managed by J. D. Frazey, who has made it during its existence of less than a year, one of the leading papers of the county. Especially was it distinguished by its able work in the late campaign, having been awarded a great deal of the honor in carrying the county for Hon. C. C. Holbrook, Republican nominee for Judge of the Twelfth Judicial District, while the county ticket was carried overwhelmingly by the Farmers' Alliance.

Moffat is the junction of the proposed Denver and Rio Grande cut-off to Creede and Southwestern Colorado. To this end were the large depot and extensive yards constructed. Moffat is destined to become one of the San Luis Valley's leading towns.

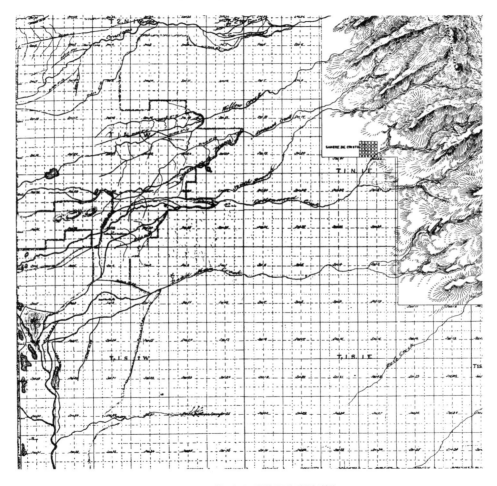

MAP OF THE CRESTONE ESTATE

THE CRESTONE ESTATE

The Crestone Estate, officially known as the Baca Grant No. 4, is delineated by the government survey maps as a rectangular plat in the San Luis Valley, County of Saguache, having for its northern boundary line the 38° north latitude. This grant of land was located by the United States Surveyor General for Colorado in the name of the heirs of Luis Maria Baca under and by virtue of an act of Congress of the United States, approved June 21, 1860.

Title was acquired by deeds of conveyance, regular and unquestionable in every respect, from the heirs of Baca, and thence through their successors. The estate was located, as provided in the act of Congress, in a body 12½ miles square, containing, as stated in the Surveyor General's certificate of location, 99,289 39-100 acres. The property is entirely enclosed by fence constructed of cedar posts and barbed steel wire, while partition fences divide the interior into eight separate enclosures, making altogether over 90 miles of fencing on the property. At the home ranch is a dwelling house, situated on the verge of a well timbered, well watered park sloping from the mountains, while herders' houses, commodious frame stable and carriage house, shops, blacksmith and carpenter shops, granaries, cattle scales, sheds and corrals for feeding and branding, wagon sheds, poultry yards, etc., cluster around the environment. On the estate are also nine camps fully equipped, at one of which is a feed corral covering ten acres and watered by an artesian well, with shedding covering an area of 46,205 square feet.

The lands of the entire estate may be classified as follows:

First a mountain and mineral division heavily timbered and richly grassed, 10,000 acres in extent, lying along the western slope of the Sangre de Christo range giving birth to seven streams, three of which are fed by great mountain lakes. In this division and the mines opened so far, gold seems to be the predominating mineral, although silver, copper, lead and iron are found in quantities sufficient to justify the erection of reduction works on the spot, and the little development so far done is rich in specimen and promise. The sloping sides of gulches and mountains are also thickly covered up to timber line with pine, spruce, fur, pinon, cedar or cottonwood, supplying the best timber for building purposes, poles for shed, fence or corral, and fuel for the fire. The second division is a middle belt of rolling prairie, irrigable land, consisting of about 60,000 acres, well grassed and cultivable at small expense from the streams and lakes on the estate. The third division embraces 30,000 acres of turf-sodded meadows, with a present annual capacity of 30,000 tons of hay. One hundred miles of irrigating ditches with perpetual rights secured by a decree of the District Court of Saguache County, web this broad expanse, while the stations Moffat, La Garita, Dune and Garrison, on the Villa Grove-Alamosa extension, provide ample shipping facilities from every point.

The native grasses consist chiefly of bunch, gramma, buffalo, wire, blue, blue joint, red top and wild clover. A fine growth of silver sage also provides fine feed after frost, and 12,000 head of stock can find pasture here the year round.

The soil is light, loamy and warm, with every necessary element for the big growths it promotes, and along the streams and on the lower lands fruits and vegetables may be successfully cultivated.

The mountain streams emerging from the canons are fringed with cottonwoods and are named as follows: North and South Crestone, Willow, North and South Spanish, Cottonwood, Deadman, Pole, Sand and the Saguache. There are also many springs and lakes, and from artesian water at a depth of from 150 to 400 feet from forty to eighty acres of land may be irrigated, while the physiological features of the estate offer every facility for the construction of reservoirs.

The estate is warm and sheltered by the big ranges that surround the San Luis Valley from the winter storms, and the light snowfall quickly succumbs to the power of Colorado sunshine.

The recent completion of the Denver and Rio Grande road from Villa Grove to Alamosa and consequent opening to easy access the markets of the north, the west and the south for the cattle, horses, hay and grain raised on the estate still further enhance its value, while the continuous demand for lumber will find in its mountains a ready and profitable source of supply.

Along the outside of the barrier of the fences of the Crestone estate the land is already all taken up by individual holders, which define the long lines of the estate with recurring sequence of stock-yard and farm-house.

TOWN OF SAGUACHE

THE Saguache Town Company filed its articles of incorporation February 20, 1874, with the following officers and trustees: President, D. Heimberger; Secretary, Geo. S. Parsons; Treasurer, A. Slone. Trustees: R. H. Jones, D. H. Dunn, I. Gotthelf, A. W. Settle and P. Hotchkiss.

The townsite selected was admirably located, lying as it does at the mouth of the valley which leads to the Cochetopa Pass, fully fifty miles distant. The land designated as the townsite is level as a floor, with a slight dip to the east, just sufficient to give admirable drainage, and this the town enjoys to-day. The principal avenues, which run east and west, are lined with stately and growing cottonwoods, and give the town somewhat the appearance of a grove. Irrigating ditches, filled with clear and sparkling water from the Saguache Creek, flow on either side of the avenues. To the resident, these little streams of water are sources of continued benefit, while to the visitor they are sources of pleasure.

Saguache is situated upon the eastern side of the San Luis Valley, and distant from Hayden Pass, in the Sangre de Christo range, fully thirty miles southeast. It is surrounded by the richest agricultural lands to be found in the Valley, and from its peculiar location (being flanked by mountain spurs on the north and south, with the mountain range far to the west), is by many said to be the warmest point in the Valley.. In earlier years, when the Indians inhabited the Valley, Saguache was the point at which they assembled in order to look up their horses which had strayed away during the winter. Here, and along the Saguache Creek, was to be found abundant feed, while all other points were deeply buried in snow.

To the west for twenty miles, to the east for fifteen miles, to the south for twenty-four miles, is to be found agricultural and hay land, second to none within the borders of this great State. Upon these lands the production of hay, grain

THE SAN LUIS VALLEY

and potatoes is so great that Eastern people look with evident discredit upon the crop reports sent out from time to time. There is little use to attempt a verification of the reports unless these incredulous people can be brought face to face with the facts. The exhibit at the St. Louis Exposition in the fall of 1890 did much to convince the eastern world that Saguache County was indeed an agricultural county. Samples of grain are being continually sent East in reply to requests made; or given to Eastern visitors. At the printing office of the Saguache *Crescent* is a large exhibit of threshed grain, and from this exhibit the samples are largely drawn.

Such is the country surrounding the town of which we write. For these many years has Saguache stood up against other and competing towns, and come off victorious. She has no railroad, but is forced to haul her imports and exports from eighteen to thirty-five miles to and from the railroads. But with all these drawbacks, her merchants pay good prices for farm produce, and sell goods as cheap or cheaper than many merchants who enjoy direct railroad communication.

Here is the place that many Eastern families have located in, and for this reason: There is the finest of lands, with water plenty, and wood for fuel free for the hauling, good business opportunities, good schools and churches and society, and more than all, health. What other boon does one need? Few places combine them to a greater extent than this immediate part of the sunny San Luis Valley. The population of the town is about seven hundred souls.

The schools at Saguache are famous throughout the entire southern part of the State, and this year the seating capacity is taxed. Here the child may be started in work in the primary department and graduated ready to enter any college in the land. The school is presided over by James M. Stevens, principal and instructor of high school; Belle Williams, teacher of the grammar school; Effie C. Smith, teacher of second primary, and Blanche McRay, teacher of the primary department.

There are three churches—Baptist, Methodist and Presbyterian, so that all who desire may enjoy divine worship. The influence of the church upon a community is admitted to be good, and Saguache is no exception to the rule.

Among the secret societies we note the Masons, Odd Fellows, and Woodmen of the World. Each has a large and enthusiastic membership, and stated meetings are regularly held. Of late the Masons and Odd Fellows have shown unusual activity.

There are two newspapers printed at Saguache, the *Colorado Weekly Herald*, an Alliance paper, and the Saguache *Crescent*, a Republican paper, and the official paper for the county. The latter paper is conducted by Mingay & Lyons.

Two hotels are conducted at this place.

The officers of the town of Saguache are: Mayor, H. M. Mingay; Trustees, B. P. Stubbs, L. S. Phillips, J. M. Ellis, F. M. Townsend, G. W. Keesey, P. W. Luengen; Clerk, Lee Fairbanks; Treasurer, O. O. Fellows.

Saguache is the county seat of Saguache County, and resident among us we have: Clerk and Recorder Charles D. Jones, and Deputy B. P. Stubbs; Sheriff, L. L. Thomas; Treasurer, Abe G. Wile, and Deputy Charles B. Phillips; Deputy Assessor, S. S. Boughton; County Judge, R. H. Jones. Correspondence addressed to any person named in either list will be cheerfully answered.

BIRD'S-EYE VIEW OF THE TOWN OF SAGUACHE

CHARLES B. PHILLIPS
Clerk of District Court and Deputy County Treasurer

CHARLES B. PHILLIPS.—A man who stands exceptionally high in the estimation of the citizens of Saguache County is the subject of this sketch— Mr. Charles B. Phillips, who has been a resident of the County ten years. His popularity, honesty and trustworthiness are amply proven by the fact that he has held the position of County Treasurer, an office to which he brought executive ability of the highest order. He is at present Clerk of the District Court, and in connection with that responsible position is Deputy County Treasurer. Mr. Phillips has a reputation for honesty, probity and excellent business judgment unexcelled in the Valley, and is one of its most responsible citizens.

B. P. STUBBS.—The gentleman whose name heads this sketch is one of the pioneers of Colorado, having arrived in the State in 1861. Five years later he was elected Clerk and Recorder of El Paso County, then as now one of the wealthiest counties in the State. In 1878 he came to the San Luis Valley, and has resided here con-

SAGUACHE COUNTY BANK

ABE G. WILE
County Treasurer, Saguache County

uary 24, 1887. Mr. Stubbs' long incumbency in the office of the Clerk and Recorder has made of him an exceptionally capable and efficient officer.

ABE G. WILE.—Chief among Saguache County's most estimable young men stands Mr. Abe G. Wile, the efficient and popular County Treasurer. Mr. Wile, although a man young in years, is an old resident of the Valley, having been tinuously since that time. In Saguache County he has been prominently identified with politics. Mr. Stubbs is a Republican. He has been Deputy Clerk and Recorder several times, first under the administration of Mr. Williams, in 1881. He was also Deputy under Clerk Bertschey, in 1882 and 1883, and under Clerk Jones, the present incumbent, since Jan- in business both in Villa Grove and in Saguache. In the former place he was a member of the firm of Wile & Lott, dealers in general merchandise, and during the years 1884 and 1885 he was postmaster of that town. Mr. Wile has the proud distinction of being the youngest man in Colorado to hold so honorable a position as County Treasurer. He is well known in all

DUNN BLOCK—DENVER BEER AND BILLIARD HALL
C. J. Schreiber, Proprietor

R. H. JONES
County Judge, Saguache County

and had much to do with establishing the town of Saguache, which was partly located on his original pre-emption claim. He was also one of the organizers and was a trustee of the town company from the time of its inception until it went out of business, and was also the first Mayor of Saguache. Mr. Jones has served the County in various official capacities, having been Justice of the Peace seven terms, was County Surveyor two terms, and is now County Judge. He was postmaster from 1886 to 1891. He was a union soldier and captain of Co. F., C. N. G., until mustered out. He was elected as a Democrat, but since has become an exceedingly prominent and influential member of the Farmers' Alliance. Mr. Jones is also the editor of the *Colorado Herald*, published at portions of the County. Where he is best known there he is best liked, and he will always be found in the front rank when Saguache's interests are at stake.

R. H. JONES.—The subject of this sketch arrived in the San Luis Valley twenty-one years ago from Carlton, Ill. Mr. Jones was one of the original settlers in the Valley,

GOTTHELF & MAYER MERCANTILE COMPANY'S STORE

decisions on intricate law points have invariably been sustained by the higher courts. By profession Mr. Lampe is a surveyor, and is a master of that profession, having followed it a number of years. Politically he is a Republican, and that he is a good one is attested by the fact that he is postmaster of Saguache, having been appointed by the present administration. Mr. Lampe has resided in the town of Saguache for sixteen years, and is therefore one of her oldest citizens.

T. M. LYONS.—If there is one thing more than another of which the people of Colorado are proud it is the public school system of the State. And the people of Saguache County have every reason to congratulate themselves on possessing public insti-

ALBERT A. LAMPE
Justice of the Peace and Postmaster

Saguache, and of which R. C. Jones is half owner and publisher, one of the best and most widely read papers in the Valley.

ALBERT A. LAMPE.—The gentleman whose name heads this sketch is one of our pioneers. He has been Justice of the Peace at Saguache continuously during the past eight years. His

INTERIOR OF GOTTHELF & MAYER MERCANTILE COMPANY'S STORE

THE SAN LUIS VALLEY

B. P. STUBBS
Deputy Clerk and Recorder, Saguache County

tutions of learning second to none in Colorado. To occupy the position of Superintendent of Schools requires rare executive ability, and a presence that will inspire respect in the minds of both pupils and teachers. Mr. T. M. Lyons, Saguache County's efficient Superintendent, possesses all these qualifications in an eminent degree. He is the youngest official in the County, having been elected to the position upon attaining the age of twenty-one years. Mr. Lyons was born in Gilpin County, on July 14, 1868, thus he is a Coloradoan to the very core.

SAGUACHE COUNTY BANK.—This popular institution, officered by some of Saguache's most enterprising and yet conservative business men, opened its doors for public patronage as a private bank in May, 1880, and was incorporated as a State bank in July, 1882, with a paid up capital of $30,000, and has since added a surplus of $30,000. It has long ago established a reputation as one of the leading financial institutions of the San Luis Valley.

It is managed by men of experience in the banking business, and its affairs are

WILLIAM W. IDEN'S LIVERY STABLE

T. M. LYONS
Superintendent of Public Schools, Saguache County

in the West to require any encomiums at our hands.

T. B. MacDONALD.—Mr. T. B. MacDonald, one of the foremost practitioners of the Valley, has followed his profession in Saguache since 1888, coming here from Medicine Lodge, Kansas, where he was a lawyer of excellent standing. He is a graduate of the Columbian Law College, of Washington, D. C., an American by birth, thirty-one years of age, and among the best read of the disciples of Blackstone in the West. His native talents and innate ability make him an adversary worthy of the steel of his opponents. He enjoys a widespread reputation as a lawyer of ability, and his practice is not encompassed by local lines. He is an affable gentleman, a fluent speaker, and

conducted with prudence and great care.

Every accommodation is granted its customers consistent with legitimate banking. The Directors of the bank are: Isaac Gotthelf, President; Leopold Mayer, Vice-President; Chas. Tarbell, Cashier; C. S. Cornelius, Assistant Cashier, and Mark Biedell, names that are too well known

GEORGE JEEP'S BLACKSMITH SHOP

T. B. McDONALD
Lawyer

reckons friends and admirers by the legion.

C. J. SCHREIBER.—The Denver Beer and Billiard Hall is owned and conducted by Mr. C. J. Schreiber, who is without question one of the most popular and affable men in the city. He conducts his place in an orderly manner, and in stock carries only the most popular lines of wines and liquors from the most celebrated vintages of the world and cigars of the best of home and foreign manufacture. He has resided here for over nine years and is everywhere known as an honorable, conservative business man.

THE GOTTHELF AND MAYER MERCANTILE CO.—The Gotthelf and Mayer Mercantile Company was first founded in 1867 by Mr. Isaac Gotthelf, who, since that time, associated with him Messrs. Leopold Mayer and Perry H. Bertschy, and they incorporated The Gotthelf and Mayer Mercantile Co. in September, 1889. The store-room of the retail department of this house is amply large to display to advantage the enormous stock carried, which consists of almost everything in the general merchandise line

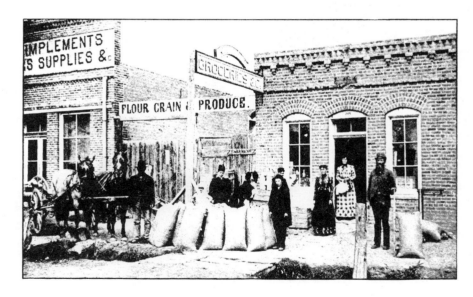

E. J. JONES' GENERAL STORE

MICHAEL WHITE
County Assessor, Saguache County

who have aided every measure for the advancement of San Luis Valley, and who combine the conservatism of the East with the push and enterprise that characterize our successful merchants of the West.

WILLIAM W. IDEN.—The Eureka Livery and Feed Stable, under the present able management of Mr. William W. Iden, is characterized without any restriction as a success. The causes are evident, for the reason that the stable is large and conveniently arranged—good ventilation, etc., and there will be found at all times, stylish turnouts of every description and polite attendants. Mr. Iden gives his personal attention to his business. He is an experienced man in his line, a fine judge of horses and understands thoroughly how to handle them,

with the one exception of hardware. It is one of the largest stocks in the State, and for quality, extent and general excellence, is absolutely unsurpassed by any contemporary house in the West. The officers of the company are: Isaac Gotthelf, President; Leopold Mayer, Vice-President, and Perry H. Bertschy, Secretary and Treasurer, gentlemen

REIDENCE OF E. J. JONES

THOMAS NOLAND
of Noland & Joy, dealers in Meat

repairing, horseshoeing, etc., and in his chosen avocation always turns out the best of work. Mr. Jeep came to this Valley in 1880, and has ever identified himself with every factor that would tend to the advancement and prosperity of this city. He has resided in Saguache for the past eleven years and is everywhere known as a genial and affable gentleman, an excellent mechanic and a business man of ability.

MICHAEL WHITE.—Among Saguache County's most prominent and trustworthy citizens—the subject of this sketch—Michael White takes front rank. He is a native of Du Page County, Ill., and has been a resident of the San Luis Valley for eighteen years, during all of

consequently, the best of animals may be had at this barn. Mr. Iden has resided in this Valley about three and a half years, two and a half of which he has spent in this city.

GEORGE JEEP.—The above named gentleman is the leading blacksmith and wagon maker of Saguache. He does all kinds of blacksmithing and

FAIRVIEW HOTEL
A. M. Hoagland, Proprietor

W. S. JOY
of Noland & Joy, dealers in Meat

the estimation of the members of that party, he never, until two years ago, permitted the use of his name as a candidate for office. Mr. White was elected to the responsible position of County Assessor by a splendid majority, thus proving beyond doubt that he is one of the most popular men in this section of the State.

E. J. JONES.—Among the representative establishments in Saguache, the one of which E. J. Jones is proprietor, and P. M. Jones general manager, certainly deserves prominent and favorable mention. Mr. P. M. Jones is a gentleman of keen sagacity and solid business principles. He has resided in this city since 1875, and it may truly be said that Mr. Jones has expended more money in the building of business blocks and residences, and done more for the upbuilding of Saguache

which time he has been a resident of this County, and has always been prominently identified with the material interests of the County. By occupation he is a farmer, and that he is a practical one is amply demonstrated by the magnificent crops he raises every year. He is a Democrat of the Andrew Jackson variety, and while he has always stood high in

NATHAN RUSSELL'S RANCH

H. M. MINGAY
of Mingay & Lyons, Publishers

BIRT CLARE.—You have of course heard of the man who was well heeled and the man with the good sole, and all have in their time been more or less on their uppers, so what more interesting subject could we have than that of the boot and shoe maker? Mr. Clare is a gentleman of well-known probity, whose six years' business experience in Saguache has gained for him friendships of the strongest kind, while his establishment ranks as a representative one. Mr. Clare is always found in the front rank of the van when the San Luis Valley's interests are at stake.

NOLAND & JOY.—Among the latest acquisitions to the mercantile arena of Saguache is the establishment of Messrs.

than any one other factor or person. Mr. Jones has a widespread reputation for integrity and business honor, and is respected by all for his square dealings and sterling worth. Although not a politician, he has had a number of offices given him, which shows the general feeling and sentiment of his fellow residents in this County.

M. WHITE'S RANCH

BIRT CLARE
Shoemaker

very strong team. They are of that metal which is coined from integrity, probity and public-spirited liberality.

J. S. GAY.—Mr. J. S. Gay has been Justice of the Peace at La Garita during the past six years. He is also the Postmaster and has been for five years, appointed by President Cleveland and re-appointed by President Harrison. Mr. Gay is one of those residents of the Valley of whom any community can justly be proud, and he can always be found with his shoulder to the wheel in any project which has for its object the advancement of the material interests of the San Luis Valley, with which he has been so long and favorably identified, having resided in the Valley for ten

Noland & Joy, who are dealers in meats. Although both these gentlemen are young men, they bring to their aid a very large acquaintance, gained through their many years of residence in this Valley. The firm is composed of Mr. T. Noland, who has resided here over thirteen years, and Mr. W. S. Joy, whose residence dates back to 1874. Together they make a

J. T. PIERSON'S RANCH

A. C. MACK
Dealer in Liquors and Cigars

pensation of liquors and cigars. There is to be found all kinds of wines and liquors, representing the most celebrated vintages of the world, and cigars which are the best of either European or home manufacture, and the establishment itself is the quintessence of all that is neat and orderly. Mr. Mack has resided in this city for the past three years and is everywhere known for those attributes of integrity and probity that make men so successful in their own localities, and with the large and well regarded acquaintance that he enjoys, he is sure to meet with much success.

NATHAN RUSSELL.—Mr. Nathan Russell is one of Saguache County's oldest and most highly respected citizens. That

years. Mr. Gay is a farmer by profession and is deeply interested in all that pertains to their future. He runs a general store and livery at La Garita, and owns a hundred head of cattle.

A. C. MACK.—Among the newest business ventures in the town of Saguache is the saloon of Mr. A. C. Mack, who but lately opened a model resort for the dis-

RANCH OF LIBRADON VALDEZ

J. B. MAROLD
Dealer in Stoves and Tinware

and substantial, and a credit to him and to the County. In the matter of stock Mr. Russell is excellently and abundantly supplied, owning a large number of cattle and horses.

LIBRADON VALDEZ. — Mr. L. Valdez came to the place over five years ago, and is now the possessor of two ranches, of 160 acres each, which are undeniably among the most attractive of the many handsome ranches of Saguache County.

D. HERBERT DUNN. — The above named gentleman came to this Valley in 1870, and out of a choice of seven places selected for his home the present location —Willowdale Ranch— comprising 320 acres of fine farming lands, so nestling in the foot-hills that it commands a view of the Valley and combines the elements of a villa home, a suburban residence

he is an enterprising, progressive farmer is evidenced by his property just outside the town of Saguache. Mr. Russell is the owner of one of the finest ranches in the entire San Luis Valley. He has nearly 2,000 acres of land, and raises an abundance of such crops as are usually grown in this section. His improvements in the shape of buildings are large

J. S. GAY'S RANCH

and a country place. Besides the Willowdale Ranch Mr. Dunn owns and conducts the La Garita Ranch, which comprises 1,040 acres, where cereals and hay are raised in large quantities. Mr. Dunn is one of those few men whom, the longer the community in which he resides know him, the better he is liked—an enterprising ranchman, a genial host and a gentleman of the old school.

J. B. MAROLD.—Among the representative business men of this city is the well known and popular Mr. J. B. Marold, who, during his eleven years of residence in this city, has gained legions of friends. He conducts a hardware store, his stock embracing everything in the line of stove and tinware of every description. His location is in the Post Office Block. Mr. Marold is one of those genial and affable gentlemen who makes a friend of everyone with whom he comes in contact.

JAMES CAMPER.—Mr. Camper came to this State over thirty years ago, and made in Gilpin County the first bread that was ever made in the State by a professional baker. He came to Saguache some ten years ago, and has determined to make this city his permanent home. His business here as a baker is growing with the growth of the city and the Valley, and is for sale.

SMITH BROS.—The above firm is composed of William H. and John Smith, and they own one of the best ranches in the Valley. They came to the Valley six years ago from Leadville, and bought relinquishments of 160 acres each from four men. Since that time they have added to their possessions until they now own 1,000 acres of deeded land, which is fenced, and have 700 acres under cultivation. They raise 400 tons of hay per year, and have 40 acres in grain for their own use. They own about 300 head of cattle and 30 horses, and in the winter feed 100 steers on the ranch. The Smith Bros. have an excellent four-room plastered

D. H. DUNN'S RANCH

house on their place, and in the yard have an artesian well 130 feet deep, with a splendid six inch flow.

J. D. WILSON.—Every old resident of Saguache County is acquainted with the subject of this sketch, who is one of the old-timers of this section. Mr. Wilson owns one of the finest ranches in the San Luis Valley, and has on his place some of the most extensive and substantial buildings. He pays particular attention to breeding fine blooded stock, and in this line is acknowledged to be foremost in the Valley. He has a large and well cultivated ranch, and raises splendid crops. Personally Mr. Wilson is a most genial and pleasant gentleman, and has made a host of friends by his upright conduct in business matters.

JULIAN T. PIERSON.—In the person of the above-named gentleman Saguache County has not only a wide-awake, energetic ranchman, but also one of the youngest in the Valley. Mr. Pierson is the possessor of some of the finest and most prolific land in this Valley, and he raises crops second to none in extent and quality. He is supplied with everything essential in the way of improved machinery, good stock and splendid buildings. Mr. Pierson is a successful young man, and stands high in the estimation of the people of Saguache and surrounding counties.

CREEDE

In the highlands drained by the Rio Grande and a short distance from Wagon Wheel Gap nestles the marvelous mining camp of Creede. Prior to 1890 it had no existence, and while the ranchmen thereabouts had some inkling of the deposits of mineral wealth, this knowledge was presumptive, being based solely upon the occasional out-cropping of low grade ore. For ten years the land of which the vast silver formation is a part was used by M. H. Wason as a range, and winter and summer his cattle nibbled a bare sus-

J. D. WILSON'S RANCH

tenance upon the hills which covered the deposits of the Holy Moses, the Last Chance, Amethyst, the Bachelor, Ridge, and the Ethel.

Captain N. C. Creede, who had been prospecting elsewhere in the mountains, learned of these rumors and in May of 1889 went to these hills and with his partner, George L. Smith, of Salida, proceeded with a systematic search. The hills are on either side of Willow creek, a tributary on the Rio Grande River, and this stream extends due north and south, eating its way through gorges the rocks of which rise 300 feet on either side of the stream. East and west branches of this stream again bisect the hills. The altitude of the country is 10,000 feet, rising rapidly from the bed of the stream to a height of 1,500 and 2,000 feet to the shafts of the bonanza discoveries. One of these hills is named Campbell Mountain, in honor of the military genius in whose hands was placed the construction of Fort Logan, near Denver. Upon this mountain Captain Creede began his work, and in a short while discovered a vein. This was located by himself and Mr. Smith, and has since become known as the Holy Moses mine. Two months later Charles F. Nelson began prospecting upon the hill and located the Ridge and Solomon mines, and these locations were followed by the discovery of the Ethel, which was located by Captain Creede.

The wonderful nature of these discoveries immediately raised the question of their durability. A study of the formation was at once made, and it became evident to these gentlemen that the mountains were what is known as the bracite volcanic. Indications of a severe glacial action are apparent upon every hand. And the further indications are that this was the action of ages. The glacial flood filled the surrounding country with the float abraded from the outcropings, and to this action is attributed the almost surface appearance of the ore bodies themselves. The first ore taken

SMITH BROS.' RANCH

BIRD'S-EYE VIEW OF CREEDE CAMP

from the Holy Moses assayed $80 a ton and carried native silver, horn glance and sulphuret or amethyst quartz, spar and talc, with an occasional occurrence of lead carbonate. A shaft was sunk, with the result of finding solid walls and a five-foot vein of ore in place.

The discoverers did some development that summer. In the spring of 1890 they returned and did more effective work. At this juncture David H. Moffat, President of the Denver and Rio Grande Railroad; Sylvester T. Smith, the General Manager, and Captain L. E. Campbell, of Fort Logan, became interested, and to them Captain Creede and Mr. Smith explained the situation and asked for capital and better shipping facilities. In the deal that followed a bond upon the Holy Moses was given by Captain Creede and his partner for $70,000, and Messrs. Moffat, Smith and Campbell became at once identified with the prospect. It was the publication of this fact that directed attention to Willow Creek and the King Solomon district. The stampede began and soon prospectors were thick upon Campbell Mountain. The purchasers of the Holy Moses put thirty men to work and the results

created a burning demand for facilities.

The question of the extension of the Denver and Rio Grande a distance of ten miles to the mine was then raised, and the bickerings to which this question gave rise were carried into the directory meetings of the company in New York. The outcome of that struggle was the resignation of Mr. Moffat from the presidency and Mr. Smith from the management of the company. The extension was refused and an independent company, the Rio Grande and Gunnison, was organized and the railroad was built. The subsequent revelations have shown that Mr. Moffat was right and the directors of the Denver and Rio Grande were wrong. While this side issue was at stake the work at the mines was continued. Plans were matured for the construction of a wire tramway that would carry the ore to the valley below, where it would be loaded upon the cars as soon as the Gunnison line completed its construction.

The Holy Moses Mining Company was incorporated about the same time, and the development that was being done dissipated the notion that the ore was simply large-bodied fissure veins. The

company, therefore, extended its purchase along the lode, and Captain Creede was employed by them at a large salary and a third interest in all subsequent discoveries. There being 100 tons of ore on the dump, the Holy Moses Company ceased development, and the construction of the tramway was pushed rapidly forward. It was soon completed, and extends to an elevation of 1,100 feet from the gulch of the creek and is 2,000 feet in length, and has a capacity of 200 tons per day.

The rapid incoming of prospectors and the discovery and development of other mines built a community of habitations the counterpart of which has no existence in this or any other mining section. Heretofore camps have been favored with a building site for a city within easy reach. With the King Solomon district it was different. By common consent the gulch of Willow Creek, at the foot of Campbell Mountain, became the abode of the embryo city. It is no wider than a street in Denver, and on either side of the stream the walls rise 300 feet. Over the stream the houses are constructed with pole foundations, to raise them above the bed. It is simply a gorge, and upon the sides the houses cling in a most precarious fashion. The dangers which this primitive mode of construction invariably produces are well understood by the miners, yet day by day they go on apparently indifferent to the catastrophe which a spring thaw is certain to produce. Over 2,000 people are crowded into this gulch, and the possibility some day of an involuntary ride upon a mountain torrent with all their belongings is the frequent topic of conversation. The undesirability of this as a site for a permanent abode has stimulated town-lot enterprises at a point half a mile below the gulch at a place known as Jimtown or Amethyst. This town abuts a section of school land, and a short distance below this is the town site of Wason, named after the ranchman whose cattle for so long held exclusive privileges over these bonanza fields. The town in the gulch was called Willow, taking its name from the stream that flowed beneath the foundations. Subsequently, it was named Creede, and the suggestions made by Governor Routt upon his recent trip to the mines will probably be adopted, and that is, to merge the three towns into one and lay out the city of South Creede on the school section which the State is to plat and sell.

That which contributed most to the more recent fame of Creede camp was the discovery made in August, 1891, on

N. C. CREEDE
Founder of Creede Camp

Bachelor Mountain by Theodore Rennica, who then had Ralph Granger, Julius Haase and Erich von Buddenbrock for partners. An outcropping of a rich mineral not dissimilar from that of the Holy Moses was found in a five-foot vein. This property was located as the Last Chance. N. C. Creede discovered the cropping about the same time and at once recognized its value. As soon as the stakes were set on the Last Chance he located the Amethyst, adjoining the first location on the north. The vein was soon found to be all that the cropping promised and two producing mines that gave ore worth $170 a ton from the first shovelful were added to the list. The excitement at once centered on this hill, and since that time hundreds of locations have been made on and along the vein and this prospecting led to the finding of many promising lodes and apparent blanket veins on Bachelor Mountain.

The Bachelor, an old location, was discovered several years ago by J. P. Burnett and passed into the hands of J. C. McKenzie, James Wilson, M. V. B. Wason and others. Soon after the discovery of the Last Chance this property was purchased by parties interested in the Holy Moses Company for $20,000, and later the Bachelor Mining Company was incorporated, with David H. Moffat, Sylvester T. Smith, Frederick F. Struby,

Julius E. French and John T. Herrick for directors, and a capital stock of $100,000. The purchasers made extended development and have made a mine of the property.

The Last Chance has had a change of ownership. The other partners soon purchased the interest of Julius Haase for $10,000, and on November 22d Rennica and Buddenbrock sold their one-third interest to Messrs. Sanders, Dixon and others for $50,000 each. It is said that Mr. Granger was offered $100,000 for his one-third a day or two after this, but refused to sell. The property has produced an immense quantity of ore, and the owners have recently contracted with Humphrey & Co. for the delivery of 100 tons a day to the railroad at Amethyst.

The Amethyst has a vein of ore about five feet wide between walls. It has been developed with two shafts located about 200 feet apart on the vein, one eighty and the other ninety feet deep. In sinking these shafts, seventy-eight carloads of ore which ran from $90 at the start and now $170 a ton, have been taken out and shipped. They are now drifting between the two shafts and are sending out from eight to ten cars a day. Not a pound of ore has been taken out except in development. It is estimated $1,000,000 worth of ore will be blocked out between these two shafts. A third shaft is now being put down, and a steam hoisting plant is soon to be added.

The ore in the Amethyst, the Last Chance and Bachelor is of the same character and all are on the one lead. It is of milling character, carrying much native silver, silver glance and some horn silver. Both quartz and talcite are the foundation. The mineral is solid between walls and is shipped without sorting. One peculiarity of these mines which old miners will recognize as a marvelous thing, they have no "dump" for the reason that there is no waste in the mines and nothing to be "dumped."

The properties of the Moses Company are all under the general management of Captain Campbell. Harry Allenby is superintendent, with James O'Brien and Samuel Billings foremen.

The Ethel May has about 5,000 tons on the dump and will work about thirty-five men. A tunnel to be about 300 feet long is being run to cut the vein considerably lower than the first working.

Ex-Senator Thomas M. Bowen purchased the Ridge and the Solomon of C. F. Nelson, and has hold of a large group comprising the Mexico and others. After holding them a few months, developing them to some extent and making important strikes in the Ridge and Solomon, he sold the group for a good round sum to George Nichol and others, who added to it by the purchase of the St. Peter, Wandering Jew, Rio Grande, Maggie and Mammoth No. 2. Considerable development is now going on, with occasional shipments. The Ethel lies in the centre of this group.

Charles Nelson holds the Yankee Girl, lying below the Moses, and has it developed with a 190-foot tunnel. He has also the Casino fraction, between the Cliff and the Phœnix.

The Lena, lying just off the Cliff, is owned by L. M. Stollard and R. W. Griswold. The Phœnix, Jr., is the property of Tom Johnson, Louis Pierce and Frank Oliver.

There are any number of good claims on the hill on which little but the assessment work has been done, and which will require much more development to bring them into pay. During the short working season of last summer much decisive work was done, but not enough to thoroughly show up the extent or nature of the mineral deposit.

From south to north on Bachelor Hill the claims lying along the vein are, first the Bachelor; parallel to it the Spar, then north comes the Commodore and Sunnyside, at the end of them the Del Monte, then the Last Chance, the Amethyst, then the Cleopatra. South of the Bachelor is another good property, the Lenore, owned by Charles Nelson and James McClurg, of Denver. East and parallel with the Cleopatra is the Daisy, owned by the Moses Company.

The Cleopatra is owned by D. S. Cotton & Co., Salida parties. It is unquestionably certain to become a shipper in a short time.

The Sunnyside is owned by A. C. Dore, and $20,000 was refused for it some time ago, while it was yet a prospect.

The Little Maid and Silver Plume are two claims on Bachelor Hill which lie north of the Cleopatra and are owned by U. F. Smith and M. C. Merrill, a banker of Kansas City. The owners are confident of getting the lead next summer.

L. F. Bradshaw, R. W. and E. P. Watson have two fine-looking claims on the big blanket lode on this mountain.

The Grant No. 1, with fifteen feet of quartz well mineralized, is one of them. They have every indication of great richness ahead.

HENRY ALLENBY
Superintendent Holy Moses Mining Company

H. P. Griswold and C. C. Cotton have a claim in this vicinity that is showing stuff similar to the Granger lode. The Grand View and Salem are some splendid prospects in this vicinity.

The Golden Eagle is a prospect to the west of the Amethyst which shows good rock and seems to be on the big blanket. It is owned by Denver parties, who will have development work done at once.

The Annie Rooney, lying southeast of the Last Chance, was located by L. M. Stollard and R. W. Griswold and purchased by the Willow Creek Mining and Milling Company, composed of Rio Grande Railroad officials. President E. T. Jeffrey is president of the company; W. R. Dietrick, J. B. Moore and M. H. Rogers are directors. It is patented ground and is considered one of the most promising in the undeveloped course of the big lead.

The Conejos, Nos. 1 and 2, located at the west side of Windy Gulch, are held by C. C. Cotton, H. P. Griswold and E. S. DeGolyer. It has a lead of talc and quartz and iron and gives assay of $30 a ton on the surface.

The New York overlaps the Last Chance, and its owners, George L. Smith and Samuel Coffin, are to all appearances preparing to make a strong fight at law for the big mine, claiming some illegal moving of stakes after the first location was made. The Pittsburgh, by the same owners, angles to the northwest from the New York.

The Del Monte was located by Chas. F. Nelson to the east of the Last Chance, which it overlaps at the south end and takes in about 100 feet of the big lead. Mr. Nelson is sinking a shaft on the property in Chinese tallow or talc, which is day by day becoming better mineralized. This work promises to be the most effective development of the big deposit which has been made outside of the mines directly on the lead, and its result is watched with a great deal of interest.

The St. Charles joins end lines with the Bachelor on the south and has a good showing for the vein.

The old giant of the camp is Mammoth Mountain. It rises bluff and ponderous above the gulch, and looks as though it might be a tower of mineral strength. A number of good prospects were opened there late this fall, and there is every reason to believe that there will be great mines opened there.

The Mammoth is a monster lode, twelve feet wide, which was located by Mr. Creede for the Moses Company.

The character of the ore is silver and copper. Systematic development will be made in the spring.

Charles F. Nelson has the Emily and the Centaur on this lode, being extensions of the Mammoth.

Thomas Hastings has a number of valuable locations on this mountain. In the Homestake he is getting gold rock that runs $13 at the surface, and is rapidly getting better, with indications of a big mine ahead. The Golden Terror, Silent Friend and Clara are also his locations.

Back from the gulch on this mountain there is an immense ledge of lime that seems to dip into the Mammoth. On this Herman Kruger is working on a shaft. He has sunk forty-six feet through a carbonate of iron and expects to find blue lime beneath it. He is from Leadville, and is of the opinion that the formation is similar to that of the great carbonate camp.

The only gold in the camp is found on this mountain. Authorities are in dispute as to the structure and lay of the mineral deposit, and it will require at least another summer's work to settle the question.

There is much ground which has yet

to be prospected and a few localities in the vicinity of the three big hills have already been staked and will, no doubt, in time be added to the shipping section. Deep Creek, Blue Creek and Hot Springs gulch, the two last named in the vicinity of Wagon Wheel Gap, have some flattering prospects. The main range has been but slightly scratched in two or three places, and these give much encouragement. Hugh Wilson has a number of good locations above timber-line and about ten miles west of Creede; and C. C. Cotton and H. P. Griswold made one location at the head of East Willow which they call the Timber-line. An immense blowout about 200 feet square makes a great showing of white quartz, the surface float rock of which gives an assay of $46 in gold and some silver. It has lead indications about it and they will make development this spring.

The Montezuma is a claim held by Cotton and Griswold on the blanket formation below Amethyst. It is an iron carbonate that gives assay of forty ounces in silver.

Winter opening up in this locality with unprecedented severity, the work of prospecting ceased and the question of a suitable location for a town attracted the attention of the miners, and disputes grew in number and vehemence through the month of December. The school section is in close proximity to the mines, and notwithstanding the fact that M. V. Wason had upon it a lease from the State Land Board, squatters entered upon the property and began to claim title upon the ground that the land was mineral, and therefore should revert to the Government. The unnumbered decisions to the contrary in the United States Land Office in similar cases did not daunt them and steps were begun to open a vigorous fight against the State.

The people not only seized upon the land for the erection of their homes, but they sunk shafts and began to open veins of mineral. The clash among the parties

W. I. COVERT
Dealer in General Merchandise

interested became so vigorous that the noise of the wrangle finally reached the ears of the Governor and the State Land Board, and early in January they proceeded to Creede in a body. It was no pleasure trip and the officials endeavored to dodge the duty, but the Governor was obstinate. They all had to go. In the party there were Governor Routt, Secretary of State Eaton, State Auditor

THE CLIFF HOTEL
Frank M. Osgood, Proprietor

Henderson, Insurance Commissioner Hurd, Superintendent Coy, State Engineer Maxwell, Attorney-General Maupin, Register France and Adjutant-General Kennedy.

The advent of the Governor was announced with such *eclat* as the limited means of the community could command. Everything that was capable of noise was brought into requisition, and the salvos that the hills re-echoed made the huge pines tremble. There was no time lost in getting down to business, and the leading citizen, in a woolen shirt, broke the trail for his excellency, whose short legs made sorry efforts in tracing the footprints. The largest edifice in the place was a general merchandise store, into which the Governor was led. Here was gathered a large number of the able-bodied men in the camp. A beer-keg, upended, was the rostrum, and upon this the Governor was raised. The speech he made was not long, nor was it particularly eloquent, but it struck the spot. He would have said more, but the physical exertion he made to maintain his equilibrium upon the keg consumed much of his reserve power. As he climbed down, however, he was heard to say: "You fellows are getting into trouble, following the advice of some jack-legged lawyer." The roar that followed almost upset the Governor, but when he was informed that the "jack-legged lawyer" was the chairman of the meeting, he comprehended the extent of his remark and the degree of enthusiasm with which it was greeted.

The substance of the address was to the effect that the State would aid rather than retard the camp, and that the school lands would be sold to the miners by lots, and that where there was mineral the State would only exact royalty. This solved the problem, and the situation became pacific.

The Governor and the State Engineer

A. H. MAJOR & CO.'S GENERAL MERCHANDISE STORE

looked over the school land, or as much of it as peeped here and there above the snow.

Since the trip of the Governor's party a greater impulse has been given the camp and arrivals vary from fifty to one hundred per day. There are two hundred carpenters at work, and as the highlands are covered with timber, houses are multiplying rapidly. There are three papers in the place and they are doing their best to extend the fame of the camp. The latest arrival is the *Creede Candle*, published by Luke H. Johnson, a newspaper man of Denver. It is an enterprising journal and is zealous in the cause. Jimtown is also a marvelous town and Wason is receiving the overflow from the two principal camps. Those who are going into the camp at this time are largely merchants.

The first stock of goods to reach Creede was brought by W. I. Covert, who for a time supplied the needs of all. There are livery stables, saloons and shops of all kinds. Since the railroad has gone into the camp prices have been greatly reduced and living there is now comparatively reasonable. There are twelve women in the camp, and these assist in operating the boarding houses and hotels. A bank has been established, of which J. D. Mabin is President and W. O. Staton Cashier. It is associated with the State Bank at Monte Vista and has a capital of $80,000.

Every person in the Camp is now awaiting the expected boom in the spring. Lots are selling in favorable locations from $200 to $1,000, and locations upon mineral land are being held at sky figures. Among the business enterprises already in operation are the following: E. C. Covert, merchandise; J. L. Pugh, livery stable; A. H. Major & Co., mining supplies; Jesse Gully, meat market; Ewing Hardware Company; Weiss-Chapman Drug Company; F. M. Osgood, hotel;

JESSE GULLEY'S BUTCHER SHOP

J. H. Hunt, liquors; Slavick & Co., Silver State Saloon; S. I. Tice & Son, Creede Hotel; Soultrey & Co., liquors; H. P. Griswold, surveying; Lewis & Foreman, cigars; Ragan & Davis, saloon; Arthur A. Miller, surveying; Gray & Mann, saloon; B. N. Campbell, carpentering; W. A. Gibson, contractor; J. D. Miracle, lawyer; Dr. H. Pratt, physician; Dr. H. Lemke, physician; Charles A. Johnson, lawyer; W. B. Glidden, lawyer; L. M. Stollard, surveyor; J. S. Meadows, wood and coal; I. R. McLeod, saloon; Holy Moses Company's office; D. W. Hoover & Co., transfer business; Menezel & Cassedy, hardware; Doc. Munson, saloon; F. R. & E. G. Miller, lumber; D. R. Smith, general stock.

According to Rand & McNally's map, Creede is located on the line between Saguache and Hinsdale County. In consequence of the unsettled condition, property owners, anxious to be on the safe side, have filed papers in both counties. When the Governor and his party were at Creede he agreed to have the matter looked into by the Board and the State Engineer, which has been done. The developments are very strange, and it is not likely that much litigation will follow. As described by the acts of 1886, forming the counties, the west line of Saguache County is placed further to the west several miles, and an anvil-shaped piece, comprising eight or nine townships, which was supposed to be a portion of the western portion of Saguache County, is really a portion of Conejos County, as described by the law, and is cut off from the main portion of that county, and is entirely separated by Rio Grande County, which is thirty miles across.

The northern boundary of Conejos County follows along the continental divide to Cochetope pass and then southeasterly to Rio Grande River. The northern boundary of Rio Grande County is very well defined by law, and leaves

COMMISSARY OF THE HOLY MOSES MINING CO.—D. P. VAN FLEET, MANAGER

Conejos County in separate pieces, and the locality in which Creede is situated is thrown into Hinsdale County apparently.

The State Engineer is looking into the matter, and says that a survey of the line, after a thorough study of the acts of the Legislature, will be necessary to locate the new camp, and he has no idea which county it belongs to. In the meantime there seems to be but one way for the claim owners to do, and that is to file their papers in both counties until the matter is settled by a survey. The State Engineer says the snow is too deep to survey now, and thinks nothing can be done before spring.

None of the county lines have ever been surveyed in that portion of the State, as it was supposed that the bounds were sufficiently described by the several acts.

Since the carbonate discovery at Leadville no mining excitement in the State has equalled the interest which the discovery at Creede has created. Everywhere Creede is the topic of conversation, and the fever has passed beyond mining circles and has penetrated the homes in the large cities. In every resort where young men are wont to gather venturesome spirits commune and from discussion the matter generally terminates in the formation of a company to "grub stake" the more hardy and sending them forth into these hitherto unexplored regions. It is this fever that is swelling Creede's population.

CHAS. F. NELSON'S HEADQUARTERS

FRANK M. OSGOOD.—The first question that the weary traveler will ask upon arriving at Creede is where the best hostelry is, and the answer will be unanimous, the "Cliff Hotel," which is conducted upon the advanced principles of the East, with the warmhearted generousness of the West. The proprietor of this house is Mr. Frank M. Osgood, who came here in April, 1891, and, with the judgment and foresight gained through former experience in mining camps, decided that Creede had a future, and he would cast his lot with it. He is so ably assisted in his business by his wife and daughter that patrons receive all the benefits of home comforts and the best of meals, so that they are always well satisfied with their lot at the "Cliff."

N. C. CREEDE.—The father of Creede Camp is N. C. Creede, and that he is one whose paternal eye is ever watchful for his child's benefit goes without saying. Mr. Creede came to Creede Camp in 1889, and met with success almost from the start, being the discover and locater of most of the rich mines in this locality. Mr. Creede is a whole-souled man, whose assistance he is ever ready to give to any measure that will help advance the interests of his camp.

W. I. COVERT.—The above named gentleman has resided in Creede since April, 1891. He is engaged in the general merchandise business, being agent for E. C. Covert, and Justice of the Peace for Howmann precinct, and that he is a leavel headed conscientious business man, is attested by the fact that all decisions rendered by him have very rarely been disputed or appealed from.

A. H. MAJOR & CO.—The largest general merchandise store in Creede is the one conducted by A. H. Major and F. Frazer under the title which heads this article. They carry a stock which is in every way adequate to the requirements of the camp and show what confidence they have in the future. They are both gentlemen of excellent business ability and will leave no stone unturned to push Creede to the front.

JESSE GULLEY.—Creede's meat is dispensed to the inhabitants by the well and popularly known Jesse Gulley, who raises nearly all the stock that he cuts up for the trade, and that is one of the reasons why the residents of that locality praise the Pioneer Meat Market. Mr.

LOFTUS & HASTINGS' SALOON

Gulley came to Creede in June, 1891, although residing in the Valley for the past twelve years. He is identified extensively with its interests, and is ever ready to place himself upon record with its future.

D. P. VAN FLEET.—The subject of this sketch is the manager and bookkeeper of the commissary for the Holy Moses Mining Company. He is also engaged in mining and has some very good claims, especially the "Sunny Side." Mr. Van Fleet has resided in this Valley for over five years, coming to Creede in September, 1890. And it will not be out of place to here add that Mrs. Van Fleet was the first lady to come to Creede to reside and the only lady who braved the storms of last winter. Mr. Van Fleet is one of Creede's most enterprising residents and business men.

CHAS. F. NELSON.—One of Creede's pioneers is the above named gentleman, who came to this locality over six years ago. He was the discoverer of the "Ridge," the "Solomon," the "Phœnix" and other valuable mining properties. He is one of Creede's most enterprising and enthusiastic residents, and is ever ready to aid and foster any proposition that will be a benefit to his city.

HENRY ALLENBY.—If you want to know anything about the country surrounding Creede, ask Henry Allenby, Superintendent of the Holy Moses Mining Company, and if the question is one that will not interfere with that Company's interests, then you may be sure of ascertaining just what you want, as no better miner or posted man resides within the gates of Creede than Mr. Allenby. At present the mines under his immediate charge consist of the "Holy Moses," "Ethel," "Mammoth" and "Amethyst." His experience dates back twenty-five years. He is just as genial and affable as he is well posted, and no better com-

JUNCTION SALOON
A. J. Farris, Prop'r

panion could you ask for to gain information and pass a pleasant hour.

LOFTUS & HASTINGS.—The above firm were the first to recognize the fact that where Jimtown is now, would be the best site for a town, and so with that forethought that characterizes men as particularly intelligent, located their establishment at that point. They carry an excellent line of wines, liquors and cigars and dispense them with an air born of metropolism. The firm is composed of William Loftus and Tom Hastings, young men who combine the push of the West with the conservatism of the East.

CLIFF SALOON.—One of Creede's most popular saloons is the one conducted by William Gray and Robert Mann, and known as the Cliff Saloon. These gentlemen located the Cliff in May, 1891, and do one of the best businesses in their line in Creede, as they are popular and genial business men.

They carry in stock a line of goods that would not reflect discredit upon the most pretentious city resorts, and can at all times be relied upon to cater to the best trade and provide the best character of wines, liquors and cigars. The gentlemen have a well-earned reputation for being among the most progressive and liberal spirited citizens in Creede, and are always to be found in the front rank when the town's interests are at stake.

JUNCTION SALOON.—The proprietor of the above named saloon is the urbane and popular A. J. Farris, who came to Creede in May, 1891, although having previously resided in the Valley for five years. The class of liquors which he is known to dispense are of the best vintages, while his cigars are of the best brands. Mr. Farris is one of Creede's most enterprising citizens.

PATTON & SON'S HOTEL
Wagon Wheel Gap

COSTILLA COUNTY

Has an area of 1,700 square miles. About 1,000 square miles of this is in what is known as the Trinchera Estate and the United States Freehold Company lands. These lands are south of Mount Blanca, east of the Rio Grande River and west of the Sangre de Christo Mountains. It is watered by Ute Creek, Sangre de Christo Creek and the Trinchera River in the northern part, near Garland, and by the Upper Culebra or San Francisco, Vallejo and Seco Creeks and the Culebra and Rio Costilla Rivers in the south. The Rio Grande River bounds the county on the entire southwestern line.

Out of the Mexican grant land mentioned above there has been sold to actual settlers about 30,000 acres, comprising some of the finest natural hay and meadow, as well as some of the best farming lands in the San Luis Valley.

The first settlement made in Costilla County was at Costilla, on the Rio Costilla, in the extreme southern part of the county. It was headed by one Charles Barbeau, the grantee or the representative of the grantee of the vast tract of land above mentioned. This Barbeau was a Canadian Frenchman, who for some service and a little money to the Mexican Government procured a title to about 640,000 acres of land.

About the same time that Costilla was settled a colony of Mexicans settled at San Luis, on the Culebra River. San Luis is the present county-seat. This settlement was made in the years 1850 and 1851. The grant was made in or about 1843. Ditches were taken out, a mill was built, and farming begun in a primitive way at Costilla and San Luis as far back as 1851. Most of the inhabitants of San Luis and Costilla are Mexicans. San Luis has a population of about 1,000 souls.

The next settlement, in 1850, was by T. T. Tobin, of Kit Carson fame, on the Trinchera, about four miles southwest from the present town of Garland. Others soon followed.

About this time the United States built Fort Massachusetts, which was about five miles north of the present town of Garland. In 1857 or 1858 Fort Massachusetts was abandoned and Fort Garland built. Some of the old Government buildings are still standing. Hon. W. H. Meyer has during the past two years remodelled some of them, and

THE SAN LUIS VALLEY

uses them as a dwelling, office and ware-room. In 1870 Mr. Meyer settled on the Zapato, a small creek coming down the west side of Mount Blanca. Mr. Meyer has been a resident of the county for more than twenty years.

About 1870 gold and iron was discovered at and near the present town of Placer, a little south and west of La Veta Pass. For a time some good paying placer mines were worked, but, being upon grant land, have never been fully developed.

In 1877 the Denver and Rio Grande Railroad was built over Veta Pass, and the old town of Garland City was built. This town was near the mouth of Wagon Creek, about eight miles east of the present town of Garland. For a time it was the terminus of the Denver and Rio Grande Railroad and was a booming town.

In 1878 the Denver and Rio Grande was extended, and most of the buildings from Garland City were moved to the present town of Hermosa, which town is in Conejos County, built on the south and west banks of the Rio Grande River, that stream being the line between the two counties.

About this time, 1878, settlement was made at different places along the Rio Grande River in Costilla County, people at that time thinking that only the natural meadow lands were worth taking. Not much change was made in the condition of affairs in this county from 1878 until about the years 1886 and 1887, when it was demonstrated that the soil and climate of the San Luis Valley was adapted to the growth of wheat. Then the San Luis Valley Canal was built, settlers commenced to take up the Government land under the United States Land Laws—which for years had been only used for grazing purposes—that was north of Alamosa and west of Mount Blanca. Since 1887 most of this 440,000 acres of land has been taken by actual settlers. Canals from the Rio Grande River have been built until there is scarcely a section of land but what it is possible to get water upon. From 30 to 50 bushels of wheat is being harvested per acre from many farms where four years ago the land was thought to be worthless. The railroad from Villa Grove to Alamosa has been built, passing through the central part of this agricultural district.

The new towns of Mosca and Garrison have been built. Mosca has a good school house, employing two teachers, a daily attendance of 50 to 60 scholars; a general merchandise store, drug store, meat market, hardware, lumber yard and coal and implement dealer, two fine hotels, a fine roller mill of 150 barrels capacity. From Mosca about ninety carloads of wheat have been shipped, going to Canon City, Denver and Alamosa. During the past twelve months one hundred carloads of lumber have been unloaded and sold here.

We have an assessed valuation of property amounting to $103,300 in this school district, where three years ago there was no school district. It was Government land, a range for cattle and the home of the coyote and the antelope.

Garrison is not far behind Mosca, and all feel that it is good to be here, having water direct from the Rio Grande River, and only having to drill from 150 to 250 feet to get unfailing artesian water. The same well, at a depth of 400 feet, furnishes sufficient water to irrigate 40 acres of land. Sub-irrigation is the mode used in all this—the northern and western portion of the county. We expect great things from this part of the Valley.

————

GARRISON

The little town of Garrison is one of the most promising of the new towns of the San Luis Valley. It is situated on the Denver and Rio Grande Railroad, twenty miles north of Alamosa, twenty-six miles northeast of Monte Vista and about thirty-five miles east of Del Norte. It is surrounded by most excellent farming land on all sides and is already doing a large volume of business. The town is now little more than half a year old, the site being surveyed in February, 1891, and the erection of the first buildings commenced in March.

Although only a few months old it is already assuming the proportions of a young city, as will be seen by the illustrations in connection with this article, which show a superior class of buildings for a new town. It is also most favorably located, being as it is in the heart of the best farming country in the Valley. The soil in this vicinity is a loose sandy loam, which easily sub-irrigates, making it an easy matter for a farmer to handle a large crop, as the time and work necessary to irrigate a crop is comparatively little. Thousands of acres of this fertile land have been brought under cultivation within the past two years, and the tide of immigration is now swiftly flowing into this immediate vicinity, and at the present rate of improvement the unimproved land will not last many months. Of course this tide of immigration brings its proportion of business and enterprise to the new town, and ever since its birth it has enjoyed a substantial growth and a lucrative business.

From Garrison may be had a magnificent view of the mountain ranges surrounding the Valley—a view of which one never tires. In almost every home in the land may be seen elegantly framed paintings of mountain scenery, executed in the best style known to art, but none

BANK OF GARRISON

can equal the original, and no scenery can be more sublime and more grand and inspiring than that which is constantly before the people of Garrison. Lofty peaks covered with perpetual snow contrast their great height and grandure with deep and dark canons. Mount Sierra Blanca, the peaks of which are 14,446 feet above the level of the sea, is eighteen miles to the east of Garrison, although it appears to be much nearer. It is the highest mountain in the State of Colorado. Its lofty snow-covered peaks and hundreds of canons and gulches stand forth in all the glories of the universe right at our doors. With the reflection of the sun upon its towering peaks, its flowing streams, its deep gulches, its forests of pine and worlds of vegetation, all the colors of the rainbow are portrayed. One has only to step to the door or draw the curtain from the window to enjoy grander and more beautiful mountain scenery than ever the pen and imagination of artist could conceive. Not only in the direction of Mount Blanca are these glorious spectacles beheld, but in every direction that one may turn may be noticed the most enchanting scenery of mountain and plain.

Another feature which will in future tend to make the town of Garrison a popular point is the San Luis Lakes, which are located a few miles east of here. These are the most beautiful lakes to be found anywhere in the West, and are quite extensive—one being about two miles wide by three miles in length, which has no perceptible inlet nor outlet. There are in the same vicinity a number of smaller lakes, and all are alive with wild game. The water is pure and clear, coming from the mountains, and they are becoming very popular resorts for sportsmen. A party of engineers came all the way from Denver to spend a week at the lakes last spring, and they are becoming more popular every day. Extensive improvements are contemplated at the lakes in the near future, which will make

GARRISON & HOWARD
Dealers in General Merchandise

them a favorite resort for boaters and pleasure seekers as well as hunters.

Taking these few advantages which nature has very considerately placed in the way of building a town, coupled with the fact that farming land tributary is the very best and produces the largest and best crops ever known in the history of agriculture, and with live, go-ahead business men to push it to the front, may the people of Garrison not be justified in the belief that their town is destined to be one of the foremost and most prosperous in the Valley? It has advantages that no other town in the Valley has or can possess.

The water for irrigating the farming land tributary to Garrison is taken from the Rio Grande River, between Monte Vista and Del Norte, and conducted through the channels of the Farmers' Union and San Luis Ditch Companies' canals. The south lateral of the Farmers' Union runs a few miles south of Garrison, the central lateral crosses the railroad one-half mile north of Garrison, and the north lateral some three miles north of that. In addition to this a private company is now constructing a ditch from the south lateral, some six or eight miles southwest of town, to the railroad within the town limits. This new ditch traverses what is known as "the ridge," a high scope of country west of town, and will be the means of irrigating a large tract of land hitherto inaccessible. But little farming is done so far on the east side of the railroad, as the ditches have not extended far enough to warrant it, but a few miles east of town are several very extensive hay ranches which find a handy market and a good trading point at the new town. With the advance of irrigating ditches goes the farmer with his plow, and in another year, or two at the outside, thousands of acres of rich land east of the railroad will be brought under cultivation, and we may safely count that a family will be located on every quarter section. When this is the

H. A. BUTTERFIELD
Dealer in Lumber and Building Material

case the country will justify and support a town of one thousand inhabitants, and Garrison is keeping pace with the progress of the country, and will, in a very few years, be a wonderful little city.

The Denver and Rio Grande Railroad Company, in building the extension of their road from Villa Grove to Alamosa, calculated well upon the importance of a town at this point and purchased twenty-three acres of land here which is used as switch yards and depot grounds. The company also has at this point a large water tank which is supplied from a mammoth artesian well, the capacity of which is 700,000 gallons per day. The well is eight inches in circumference and over 700 feet deep. The writer hereof has been shown the prospectus of the depot which the company will erect here in the near future, but we are at liberty to say only that it will be one which will express confidence in the future of the town and be a credit and an ornament to a town of greater proportions.

The business men of Garrison are alive, enterprising and energetic and worthy of special mention in these pages.

THE GARRISON TOWN COMPANY is composed of a number of the wealthiest and most substantial business men in the Valley. Mr. E. H. Shotwell, President and Manager of the Town Company, came to the Valley about sixteen years ago and has the honor of being one of the pioneers who, regardless of the jeers of his fellow men, contended that the San Luis Valley would produce good grain, and to demonstrate it built ditches at his own expense and planted a few acres to grain. He was successful, and the fact being once demonstrated, capitalists took hold of the irrigation question, built large canals, with the result that the San Luis Valley is now one of the richest farming valleys in the world.

Mr. J. D. Maben, Treasurer of the Town Company, is President of the State Bank at Monte Vista, also President of the Bank of Garrison, two very substan-

COMMERCIAL HOTEL,
A. M. Burson, Prop'r

tial institutions, representing a capital of something over $80,000. Mr. Maben is a man who has been eminently successful in his business life, is far-sighted and knows a good thing when he sees it. He owns a number of shares of stock of the Town Company and also several fine farms in the vicinity.

Mr. H. H. Marsh, one of the Directors of the Town Company, is one of the wealthiest men in the West. He came to this Valley several years ago from California, and the altitude, climate, and general prosperity of the country pleased him and he made extensive investments here. Besides a number of the finest ranches in the Valley he owns a great deal of property in Monte Vista, some of which is illustrated in this book. He has great faith in Garrison, which accounts for his having invested heavily in stock of the Town Company and also in farm lands in the immediate vicinity.

The other members of the Town Company are also men of means and good judgment, who are determined to spare no effort to push the town to the front and make it in the near future one of the best towns in the Valley.

THE BANK OF GARRISON.—The lead-

THE GARRISON TRIBUNE
Danford & Hitchcock, Proprietors

ing and perhaps most important business institution is its bank, of which every citizen feels justly proud. This bank is associated with the State Bank, Monte Vista, (capital $80,000), and was opened for business in the early part of November. Mr. J. D. Maben is President and Mr. W. O. Statton Cashier. Besides furnishing a safe and convenient place for deposit and medium of exchange, it speaks to the world of the confidence placed in the town by men of capital and good business judgment. Mr. Statton, the Cashier, is a young man who came to the Valley a few months ago from Ogden, Iowa, made some investments in real estate and was so well pleased that he at once decided to make Garrison his future home. The bank, although just starting, is having a very flattering business.

GARRISON & HOWARD occupy the John Mitchell brick building with a complete stock of general merchandise. They are the pioneer merchants of the town and are having a deservedly good trade. Mr. William Garrison, the senior member of the firm, formerly owned the town site as a homestead, and dealt extensively in stock, having at one time owned a large ranch in Texas. Being desirous of seeing his homestead converted into a thriving town he sold to the Town Company, reserving only one block for his home. Mr. Herbert Howard, junior member of the firm, has had many years experience in mercantile lines, having spent his youth in a large establishment in Texas. He is a thorough business man, commands the friendship and esteem of the numerous customers of the firm, which is doing a very satisfactory business. This firm also employs the services of Mr. C. V. Hinkle, a very exemplary young man whose deportment and good standing in the community bring good cheer and patronage to his employers.

H. A. BUTTERFIELD supplies Garrison and a large portion of the Valley with lumber and building material. He formerly owned a large ranch near Monte Vista, and recognizing in Garrison, the infant, the features of a large town, he sold out and engaged in the lumber business in the new town. He carries a large and complete stock of everything in the line of building material. He has one of the neatest and most conveniently arranged offices we have seen, and keeps his stock, both in the yard and in the sheds, well arranged, clean and neat.

THE GARRISON TRIBUNE.—Another institution of which the people of Garrison have just reason to feel proud is their newspaper, *The Garrison Tribune*, one of the brightest, cleanest, and best edited local papers in the Valley. *The Tribune* is published by Danford & Hitchcock, the editorial and business management of the same being under the direction of Mr. C. M. Danford, who has had some eighteen years experience in the newspaper and printing business. The paper was established in April, 1891, and its neat appearance, spicy local and editorial columns soon won for it the favor of the people, and to-day it stands as one of the leading papers of the Valley. *The Tribune* office is well equipped with material and presses and

ELBERT HOWARD'S GENERAL MERCHANDISE STORE

has a snug little home of its own.

F. C. HITCHCOCK, who is associated with Mr. Danford in the publication of *The Tribune*, is manager of the real estate firm of Danford & Hitchcock. Mr. Hitchcock recently came to Garrison from Western Nebraska, where he was engaged in business. He was formerly engaged in the banking business at Gibbon, Neb., and while in that State was admitted to the practice of law. He is now doing a lucrative real estate business in Garrison with most flattering prospects for the future.

A. M. BURSON is proprietor of the Commercial Hotel, where the weary traveler can always find a comfortable room and a good meal. He has a large and nicely furnished house which is conducted in a pleasing manner. Mr. Burson also has large real estate interests in the vicinity of Garrison.

ELBERT HOWARD conducts another large and well stocked general merchandise store. He came to the Valley about a year ago for his wife's health, and was so well pleased with the country and prospects that he decided to cast his lot with Garrison almost as soon as the town was surveyed. He was one of the first citizens of the town, and for several months used what is now his ware-room for a store building. His business soon demanded more room and he was compelled to build a store-room 25x60 feet, using his old store for a ware-room. He carries a complete stock of general merchandise and is having a deservedly good trade.

W. A. BUELL is the village blacksmith. He came here from Texas in the early part of the summer and built a blacksmith shop and residence. He is a master workman, both in iron and wood, and commands trade from a large territory.

MILES BROTHERS are proprietors of the Garrison Livery and Feed Stables and also the Garrison Meat Market. They have a very commodious barn, well stocked with good horses and new bug-

W. A. BUELL'S BLACKSMITH SHOP.

gies; also keep hay and grain for sale. In their meat market they keep fresh meats and game, and keep a wagon on the road which supplies the country for miles around.

TABOR & ELTINGE have a large vegetable cellar and buy grain, hay, potatoes and all kinds of farm produce, for which they always pay the highest cash prices. They now have over 100,000 pounds of potatoes in their cellar.

CHAPIN & MILLER are the carpenters who have built most of the buildings now in Garrison. They are master workmen at their trade and never have any idle time. They have a very neat and commodious shop, equipped with all the modern tools used in their trade.

JOHN MITCHELL is the plasterer and brick mason who is largely interested in Garrison. He has a ranch adjoining the town site, owns the brick building occupied by Garrison & Howard and has the foundation for another building beside it. He is assisted by Mr. Charles Bisby, also a master mason, and both have been kept very busy the past season to take care of the work in the town.

SCHOOLS, CHURCHES, ETC.—Garrison, like all new towns, is not yet supplied with school and church buildings, but has very creditable organizations of that character.

The Garrison public schools occupy the hall over the Bank building and are presided over by Prof. F. S. Richardson. The school is largely attended and much interest taken by pupils, patrons and teacher.

The M. E. Church Society has an organization numbering about twenty members and hold services every two weeks in the hall over the bank. Rev. C. W. Simmons is the pastor in charge. Auxiliary to the Church Society is a Sunday-school which meets every Sunday under the supervision of Mr. J. A. Alexander. The average attendance is about forty, which is divided into five classes.

The Young People's Society of Christian Endeavor is also represented by a strong organization, which meets every two weeks and is a means of doing much good in the way of turning young minds.

Auxiliary to the public schools is a literary and debating society which meets every Saturday evening.

MESSRS. MULLEN & CO., proprietors of the Alamosa Flouring Mills, have an agent to buy grain at this place and are shipping large quantities to their mill. This firm expects to put up an extensive elevator and mill here next year.

MOSCA

Of all the towns in the great San Luis Valley Mosca is most happily situated and has the highest prospects for the future. The nearest town of any consequence—Alamosa—is fifteen miles distant. It is situated in the very heart of the great and celebrated sub-irrigation section, and is surrounded by the finest agricultural lands in the valley, the equal of which do not exist in the great West. Although but a year old Mosca is the largest town in Costilla County, and is the largest town on the Denver & Rio Grande Villa Grove extension. It does nearly double the amount of business of any other shipping point.

THE MOSCA TOWN COMPANY is composed of men of well-known business sagacity, who, recognizing the fact that there must be a town of importance in this region, determined to secure the right location and establish the town on the right

BIRD'S-EYE VIEW OF MOSCA

principles. That the best location was selected no one familiar with Mosca's surroundings can deny, situated as it is in the center of the best agricultural district in the Valley, if not in the State, being near to, and having direct railroad communication with great mining districts, both north and south; located directly on the line of Mosca Pass, by which route the coming railroal will enter the Valley, we predict that Mosca is to be the metropolis of the Valley.

The local management of the Company's affairs has been from the start in charge of Messrs. Terry & Oviatt, and to them is due much credit for the admirable manner in which its affairs have been conducted.

Lots are sold at a low price and on easy terms, and any one seeking a new home or desirous of establishing a business in a growing town, will make no mistake in locating at Mosca.

EDUCATION.— Last spring a commodious school-house was erected, which was supposed to be sufficiently large to accommodate all the pupils of the district for several years, but owing to the rapid growth of the town and vicinity, increased accommodations will soon be required. The school population has more than quadrupled during the last year, which is a greater increase than the most sanguine expected. The school board is composed of persons who are wide awake, intelligent and progressive. Their watchword seems to be "Excelsior!" They have verified this by supplying modern conveniences and appliances, by selecting teachers specially adapted to school work, and by adopting a thorough and practical course of study, including an excellent High School course. There are already classes in all the grades, including the High School; the pupils are doing excellent work, and the schools are considered pre-eminently the best in

THE MOSCA ROLLER MILLS

the county. A musical graduate drills the pupils in the theory and practice of singing.

A literary society meets every week. It is composed of a goodly number of old and young people, who are using this opportunity of self-improvement. This society is wielding a good influence on the community.

RELIGION.—A deep religious sentiment prevails in this community. Church services are held regularly twice every Sunday, and they are well attended.

A Sunday-school is kept up in a flourishing condition. It is well attended by children, by young ladies and young gentlemen and by elderly persons.

The young people consider their Society of Christian Endeavor *the best*, and invaluable as a means of spiritual growth. Their social needs are not neglected, as a series of monthly sociables are held in which interesting and profitable literary and musical programs are carried out.

SOCIETY.—The best class of American citizens are found here. They are capable, industrious and prosperous; are intelligent, cultured and refined. No better society can be found anywhere than here, not even in the most conservative circles of the East.

There are no influences here to lead the unwary astray, to destroy character or blight the happiness of home. This is a prohibition town. No saloons will ever sap and destroy the life-giving qualities of good society and happy homes.

REASONS WHY THIS LOCALITY IS DESIRABLE FOR A PERMANENT HOME.

Healthful climate.—This vicinity is noted for its extreme healthfulness and its invigorating atmosphere. It is a good place to recover health and to keep it.

Picturesque scenery.—Man can not help being elevated in his appreciation

HATHAWAY DE ARMAND'S GENERAL MERCHANDISE STORE

of the true and beautiful by beholding the grand, the inspiring and the sublime mountain scenery which surrounds us. To the east for a distance of over a hundred miles, the serried and snow-capped Sangre de Christo range looms up above the clouds, culminating in Mount Blanca, the highest point in Colorado. To the south, dome after dome lifts its lofty head into view. Westward is the main axis of the Rockies with its wonderful and magnificent scenery. In this beautiful background appears Mount Lookout, standing out in full view, crowned by a fine Observatory of the Presbyterian College of the Southwest. North, we see towers, domes, arches, lofty monuments and scenery too beautiful to be described by man.

The San Luis Lakes.—The largest lakes in Colorado are found within six miles of Mosca. This is a paradise for the hunter. Ducks, geese and other birds are found here by the millions. There is a plan on foot to make these lakes a summer resort with rapid transit from Mosca, the nearest town. In case such is done, parks, hotels and all things needed to make this a first-class summer resort will be provided.

Cheap homes.—While this part of the Valley has settled up well, yet land is cheap, comparatively, and the terms of purchase are easy. Good land, with perpetual water by irrigation, can be obtained at $10 to $15 per acre. This land will doubtless be worth from $25 to $50 per acre in a short time.

Abundance of water.—There is an abundant supply of water to this vicinity for all agricultural and other purposes. There are three large irrigating canals within three miles of Mosca, two of these being within a half-mile of town, and numerous artesian wells in and about Mosca. The construction of these wells is cheap, as the soil is soft and the water is shallow; the flow is strong and permanent, and the quality of the water is excellent for all purposes.

Cheap water.—Perpetual water-rights are much cheaper here than at most other places. These can be obtained at from $200 to $800 per 160 acres for perpetual use, on reasonable terms.

Easy irrigation.—The relief of the land is such that it can be irrigated by little labor. The land slopes slightly and uniformly to the east, just enough to be best fitted to irrigation.

Sub-irrigation.—Owing to the peculiar structure and composition of the soil, the land fills with water readily, and after a few years' artificial watering, little or no water is needed. The water can then be transferred to other land or sold.

Amount of land handled successfully.—Any person can handle more land here successfully than at most other places, owing to the condition of the soil, the lay of the land and the improved machinery used. It is a good place to make a living easily.

The soil is a rich, sandy loam and is very productive.

Crops are sure.—The abundance of water, no drought or hot winds, no hailstorms or cyclones, make this a place where people are not uneasy on account of failure of crops. No failure has ever been known in the Valley in the oldest settlements where water has been supplied sufficiently. There are always good crops.

The markets are good and convenient.—The numerous mining camps and lumbering mills in the mountains near us, and the large hay ranches in the foothills supply a good demand for our productions, and the railroad connections with all parts give us foreign markets.

Mosca is a growing town with almost all lines of business represented. Where can another town be found, of Mosca's size and age, where there is not a single unoccupied residence house, and where every tenement house and public building is owned by the one who occupies it?

A home.—Who would not enjoy living in this land of health, beautiful scenery,

CHRITTON & GOODNER'S LUMBER YARD

cheap lands, easy irrigation, sure crops, and every desirable social, educational and religious advantage?

MOSCA BUSINESS HOUSES.—Mosca has a good business representation, and it is a noteworthy fact that every man who is engaged in business here is doing well and making money. Chief among the business enterprises is the

MOSCA ROLLER MILLS.—This mill is the largest in the San Luis Valley, if not the southern part of Colorado. Built for a 750 barrel capacity, it has at this time only machinery for manufacturing 150 barrels per day. All the modern and improved milling machinery may be found in this magnificent structure. It was built by one of the best millwrights in the United States, and from the first, commenced manufacturing the finest grade of flour in the country. It has but few equals and no superiors. G. W. E. Griffith, of Denver, a gentleman of wealth and financial standing, is the chief stockholder in this enterprise. Foreseeing the future of this section as a grain producing country, he built his mill with a view of adding additional machinery as the supply of grain increased. In a few years a half-dozen such mills will hardly be able to handle the immense yield of grain. This year, within a radius of eight miles of Mosca and tributary to it, over one million bushels of wheat, oats and barley were grown, and this amount will increase 30 per cent each year for the next ten years.

HATHAWAY & DE ARMOND, dealers in general merchandise, conduct one of the largest mercantile establishments in the San Luis Valley. The firm is composed of Hon. S. W. Hathaway, member of the State Legislature, and J. C. De Armond, both of whom are old and staunch citizens of this section. Their business for the past year will amount to more than $75,000, and increases rapidly with the growth of the country. Their

THE VENDOME HOTEL
Conducted by Mrs. Lulu Small

stock is complete and has been selected with great care as to the demands of the people.

LIGGITT & CO. have the largest drug establishment in the county, and are doing a most excellent business. In connection with a full line of drugs and medicines, this firm also carries a good stock of fancy and toilet articles, books, stationery, notions, etc. Dr. R. L. Liggitt, a skilled physician and surgeon, is a member of the firm, and has a practice that reaches to all sections of the surrounding country. He came here from Berthoud, this State, and is recommended highly as a physician.

CHRITTON & GOODNER, proprietors of the Mosca Lumber Yard, were the first business men to locate at Mosca. The firm is composed of Major J. W. Chritton and James A. Goodner. They are among the most enterprising firms in the county, and by their square dealing, have sold over 150 cars of lumber and coal in less than a year. Major Chritton is owner of the famous Chritton ranch, which has become quite celebrated by reason of the enormous yield of grain which has been grown upon it.

W. H. TERRY conducts the largest livery and feed barn in the county. He has his barn well stocked with good horses and turnouts, and does a good business.

MOSCA'S NEWSPAPER.—*The Herald*, edited and published by John H. Bloom, is a live, progressive newspaper, and is recognized as one of the leading journals of the Valley. It is the official organ of the county, and has a large circulation. It is a five column quarto, and is published on Fridays. The subscription price is $1.50 per year, and persons desirous of obtaining more complete information of Mosca and the Valley, can avail themselves of no better way than by subscribing for it.

HARDWARE.—Mosca has a hardware store which does a fair business.

HOTELS.—Mosca has two hotels, the

SCHOOL HOUSE

Vendome, conducted by Mrs. Lulu Small, and the Stewart House. Both of these public hostelries do a good business and are equal to the best hotels on the line of the Denver and Rio Grande Railway between Alamosa and Salida.

TERRY & OVIATT, agents for the Mosca Loan Company, also deal extensively in real estate and insurance. They have a good list of lands which it will be safe for the land hunter to consult before purchasing.

D. E. REPSHER is a live, rustling real estate dealer who has a list of choice lands, relinquishments, etc., and is at all times pleased to show the home-seeker and land hunter over the country.

ASAY & CRANDELL, Real Estate agents, also do a good business, and have one of the largest lists of any real estate firm in the Valley.

JOHN B. WOODWORTH, Real Estate dealer and Notary Public, does a good business in his line. He also does conveyancing.

H. M. McCLURE maintains in Mosca the finest tonsorial parlors to be found between Alamosa and Salida. He is a thorough artist and makes it a business to please his customers.

BOOTS AND SHOES.—Mosca has a boot and shoe shop which manufactures boots and shoes and does all kinds of repairing.

EVAN MOORE, proprietor of the Mosca Blacksmith and Wagon Shop, carries in addition to this business, a complete line of agricultural implements. Repairing of all kinds receives prompt and special attention at this establishment.

FURNITURE.—Silas Hockett has just opened a large and complete stock of furniture, etc. This is the only exclusive furniture establishment in the county.

CARPENTERS.—Mosca is well represented with first-class carpenters and mechanics, among whom are J. M. Pulliam, W. L. Harrison, Sam Southworth and S. McLin.

CONEJOS COUNTY

WAY back in the fifties, there came northward from New Mexico a small band of colonists whose swarthy features showed the traits of the race that has its origin in the sunny land of Spain. And with them came too, men of Northern blood; leaders of the pilgrimage. Chief of the party was Major Head, Territorial Ex-Governor of Colorado, who still lives to remember those old days when with ox-teams and mule-teams, ponies and jennets, wives and children, flocks and herds, he conducted to the promised land of the San Luis Valley, the people among whom his lot had been cast.

Over the long sandy prairies of New Mexico, where no water is found; through the dreary monotony of the pinon forests; across the black mesa which stretches from the feet of San Antonio, they came at last to the sparkling waters of what is now called the Conejos River, where the rich vega lands, and the upland mesa slopes, offered a pleasant abiding place for their families, a rich pasture for their sheep and kine. Here they settled and built a town which they called Guadaloupe, "the River of the She-wolf." The town grew, the people prospered, wild game abounded in spite of catholic slaughter by the wandering Utes, but of all the undomesticated animals which ranged those wild plains, the cottontail rabbit was most abundant, most prolific. And when the new town ultimately took up permanent quarters it was called Conejos, the Mexican word for "rabbit." Years and years passed away, Colorado became a State, the great San Luis Valley was divided into four counties, and the little plaza of Conejos gave its name to one which is not the least among the big four.

But there were still no railroads, no newer progressive production of science or mechanics in Conejos County. The settlers were a people to themselves. There was a time of shearing when wool laden wagons started on the long trip over the mountains to Denver; there was a time of harvest and threshing when sheep, goats or ponies, driven round and round in the circle of a corral, shattered out more or less tainted grain. All was primitive, pastoral, patriarchal. But Governor Hunt and the then management of the Denver and Rio Grande Railroad, the little "Baby" road, endeared to all pioneers of Colorado, determined to climb over the mountain ranges into the fair Valley of San Luis. Hovering for a short time at Fort Garland, the iron horse at last crossed the Rio Grande.

Alamosa became an embryo city, the prosperous future of Conejos County a certainty.

Nearly forty years have passed since the first settlement. The old order of things has given place to the new. The uneventful life of a sequestered spot shut out from the world, far from the madding crowd, has given place to the busy hum of progressive Americanism.

Conejos County to-day scarcely knows itself. A few decimated coyotes still howl the requiem of the desert days. Chico and greasewood have given place to the hasty growth of grain fields, the prolific yield of nutritious roots. Hundreds of miles of fences enclose bush meadows and dainty pastures.

The Rio Grande, no longer permitted to hurry through irresponsive banks, is diverted into canals whose laterals irrigate thousands of acres of fertile farms. Nestling in the shade of groves of alamos, hundreds of happy homes shelter a prosperous community. Church spires and school house campaniles offer surer landmarks than the gnarled limbs of lone cottonwood trees, which once were the only signs for the adventurous traveler. The artesian well development has taught the people how to utilize the vast

GEORGE A. WILLIS
Real Estate and Insurance Broker, Alamosa

reservoir of water, which, rushing down from the melting mountain snows, and losing itself in the softness of the sand, encounters the impervious clay beds and gushes up again to the sunshine and utility when tapped under the "chug chug" of the drill. Conejos County to-day has greatly changed from the old Guadaloupe days. Parched chameleon colored corn and the narrow bosom of the native sow have given place to different delicacies. Hamlets have developed into towns; towns into cities. In the low lying mountain ranges, the hills have given up their mysteries and their wealth to the pick of the miner. Fenced fields provide the Spanish rabbits of the county with succulent supplies. Disgusted antelope look wonderingly at barbed wire enclosures. Trout and duck provide the angler and the hunter with the spoils of rod and gun.

To get down to detail, Conejos County is bounded on the west by the mountain of Platoro, rich in mineral wealth; on the east line, the waters of the Rio Grande run through twists and curves from which the great canals of the T. C. Henry companies draw a constant, never failing supply. On the north, the prairie imperceptibly merges into the spreading acres of Rio Grande. On the south, Northern New Mexico, with its barren mesas and presiding peak of San Antonio, dozes in the horizon of the San Luis Valley. The assessor's returns for 1890 give the following facts: 1,530 square miles in the County; acres of agricultural land, 147,129; miles of railroad, 74; horses, 3,816; mules, 215; asses, 45; cattle, 7,015; sheep, 11,205; swine, 558, and a total assessed valuation of $1,844,469. The soil is a rich, sandy loam. Every acre responds with the certainty of splendid crops to the sure system of irrigation. Wheat, barley and oats give immense returns of unsurpassed quality. Potatoes, vegetables and small fruits flourish in perfection. The climate is warm and sunny. Cool breezes from mountain and river temper the heat of summer, and the winter snowfall seldom outlasts two sunrises. Farming in Conejos County, as everywhere in Colorado, is by irrigation, but here, almost more than anywhere, irrigation has been reduced to a science. Men of capital and enterprise have taken from the Rio Grande immense canals from which run hundreds of miles of laterals and sub-laterals to contiguous farming lands. Artesian wells with reservoir annexes supplement the supply, and from one well alone, forty acres can find necessary water for purposes of cultivation. The increasing moisture of the soil, due to bringing to light the hidden under-flowing of the creeks, has already done away with much of the manual labor of irrigation, for seepage from parallel ditches one hundred feet apart, is on very many farms now found amply sufficient to meet the demand. The Rio Grande Del Norte, "big river of the north," finds profitable supplement in the creeks which run down from the western hills. The Alamosa, Conejos and La Jara creeks furnish to thousands of acres prolific incubation and conception of vast fields of waving grain. As for cattle, sheep and the finished product of scientific productions of live stock, few counties can compare with Conejos. The massive Percheron, the pale faced Hereford, the lithe limbs

THE ALAMOSA CLUB BUILDING

of the Cleveland bay, the rounded quarters of the Shorthorn, and the compact build of the Galloway, all find their representatives.

At La Jara, Dan Newcomb runs one of the bigest dairy farms in the State; John Harvey has a herd of Percherons and Cleveland Bays which cannot be surpassed even on their native heath; Senator Adams has cattle whose well filled hind quarters are more than suggestive of appetizing beaf steaks, and Oscar Wilkins has thousands of tons of hay which find market of merit in the home trade and the big demand of the mining camps. Many another ranch too, in this sympathetic climate, produces in long reaching stacks, the cured product of wild and tame grasses, and under the Southern sun, potatoes, rutabagas, turnips, and every root crop swell luxuriantly to gigantic proportions.

Mineral is found in all the hills which bound the western limit of the county, and recent rich discoveries have centred the interest round Platoro, where at least two mines, the Merrimac and the Mammoth, have shipped ore which challenges the competition of this mining State.

The seven thousand inhabitants of Conejos County owe a great debt to T. C. Henry of Denver. Through his enterprise companies have been formed which now own or operate some 30,000 acres of land, all fenced, and practically all brought under cultivation. The Excelsior Farm Company has under fence 17,000 acres; of this area, 8,000 acres have this year made a return of thirty bushels of wheat to the acre. The Empire Farm has 5,000 acres, farmed by 200 tenants. There are artesian wells on every quarter section. The acreage under cultivation has increased from 1,500 in 1887 to 4000 in 1891, and the yield per acre runs all the way from twenty to forty bushels of grain. A picked acre on this farm, surveyed and measured by County Surveyor Jones, yielded last year 858 bundles as large as a Deering could bind, and threshed out

THE MASONIC BLOCK, ALAMOSA

the phenomenal result of eighty-eight and two-third bushels, machine measure. The great Empire Canal furnishes water for these lands. It is calculated that its capacity is sufficient to redeem 150,000 acres of heretofore desert lands. It carries at present 2,500 cubic feet of water per second.

But the Henry companies are not the only factors which contribute to the prosperity of the county. The Mormon emigration from Utah has made out of the deserts of La Jara a grain garden. Their co-operative, scientific farming has made a model for an ambitious following. No crops are better than the crops of the Mormons of Manassa and Sanford, no steers are fatter, no horses show more the sleekness due to care and knowledgeable attention.

Conejos County may boast of a population which can well compete with the intelligence of any county in the State. As for the towns of the county, Alamosa is the chief, just as her central position must necessarily make her the chief of the towns of the Valley of San Luis. Situated on the banks of the Rio Grande, avenues of trees enfile her streets. Every citizen has done his best in this favored climate to beautify and adorn not only his residence, but his place of business. Every day new projections are formulated, every day new buildings attain completion. The corporate limits are one square mile. The electric light illumines the streets, the stores carry the latest and the best, and every citizen confidently anticipates a still increasing prosperity. Large and commodious buildings provide accommodations for the immense railroad traffic from the South and South-west. Headquarters of the fourth division of the Denver and Rio Grande Railroad, the clang of hammer and anvil is never silent in the machine shops. The lines from Fort Garland, Del Norte, Denver and Durango centre here. The water supply comes from all the purity of a hundred artesian wells; there are schools, churches and armory hall and an opera house. The passenger, freight, express and telegraph business, amounts to an average of $20,000 per month. The town is growing rapidly. Houses are going up on all sides and are rented almost before the foundations are laid. There are fifty business houses, four churches, a high school, two newspapers, a club house, six hotels, and two

FIRST NATIONAL BANK, ALAMOSA

flourishing banks. But of all the important interests contributory to Alamosa, must be mentioned the Alamosa Mill and Elevator. Modestly erected by far-seeing capital for a modest supply of grain, the almost unexpected development of the country has called this year for an increase of facilities, which now not only calls for the grain to manufacture 300 barrels a day, but also finds itself at that large capacity, almost inadequate to deal with its consignments. At the same time the quality of the flour, from the hard milling wheat raised in the adjacent country, has been found so satisfactory that the finished product is rapidly earning a deserved pre-eminence.

The estimated population of Alamosa is 1,200. The largest buildings are the Masonic and Odd Fellows halls, the Manders, Frank and Ball blocks. The Masonic order has sixty members; the Odd Fellows forty. Among contemplated improvements are a woolen mill, tannery and brewery.

Of the other towns in the county, Antonito, on the Denver and Rio Grande line, distant only one half mile from its sister city, and county seat of Conejos, calls for principal attention.

Antonito, with a population of 500, has three churches, a large brick school house, twelve stores, a newspaper and most commodious hotel quarters. The town is surrounded by a farming and sheep growing district, fertile and productive. It is headquarters for supplies to ranches, sheep camps, and the busy saw mills which carve into lumber the fragrant timber of the pine woods of New Mexico. During the year, 200,000 sheep are shipped from this point, and half a million pounds of wool change hands. Grain, potatoes, hay and other farm products are shipped in all directions, and recent government appropriations for opening roads and bridges will still further open up avenues to commerce. Almost bound by buildings to Antonito, is Conejos, the original settlement, the

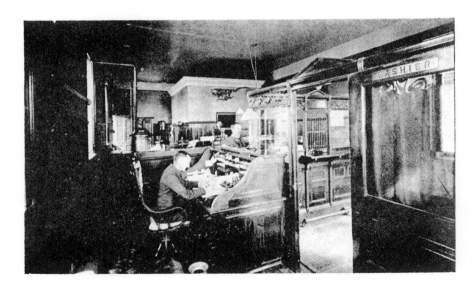

FIRST NATIONAL BANK, ALAMOSA—INTERIOR VIEW

present county seat. Here, among the adobe homes of a Mexican population, towers the court house, built of the pink and white stone furnished by the quarries of the neighborhood. Forty thousand dollars have been expended in an erection which is a credit to the county. Here, too, is the cathedral of the Catholic Church, to which is annexed the Sacred Heart Academy, still and ever doing excellent work for progressive education. Nine miles north-east of Conejos and near the Conejos River, are located the prosperous Mormon towns of Manassa and Sanford. The two settlements have a population of some 2,000, and occupy a large area, as each family have a couple of cultivated acres in its environment. An immense amount of farm products respond each year to the magic wand of skill and hard work. There is here, too, a church and school house which hold no title to the improvements of Conejos County.

Northward again, at La Jara, is a pretty village, built up by agricultural surroundings. The great horse ranch of John Harvey; the rich pastures of D. Newcomb's dairy farm; the flowery meadows of Judge McIntire, all contribute to the welfare of a town which has a right some day to a widely credentialed recognition.

Many another little town, with its tree-embowed houses, makes Conejos County picturesque. Las Sances, Capulin and Cecinero, and here and there lots of other unsuspected little communities surprise the stranger. Platoro and Stunner arrogate their claims to the richness of the mineral of the hills. No building material has ever equaled the pink and white stone, butter to carve, iron to endure, of the Conejos quarries. From the grain fields of Conejos comes to the flour mill, load after load of grain. In corral and hay-mow are stored thousands of tons of fragrantest hay. In Conejos County, pastures stand knee deep in the bush grass; flocks and herds whose better

BANK OF ALAMOSA

blood has already forgotten a hairy or long horned ancestry.

And in the cities, towns or plazas of Conejos County dwell communities intelligent, harmonious and progressive. Over all shines a sun to be envied by the blue skies of Italy.

ALAMOSA

The fair city of Alamosa, so christened from its cottonwood trees, by the poetry of the Spaniard responds with leafy wealth and slipping stream to the idea which inspired the conceit. In the centre of the heart of the San Luis Valley, on the southern bank of the Rio Grande River where it glides between the counties of Costilla and Conejos, Alamosa is fed by a thousand fertile farms and populated by a liberal, far-seeing and enterprising people. The headquarters of the fourth division of the Denver and Rio Grande Railroad are situated here, and the striking and clanging of iron on iron resounds from the machine shops. The line from Pueblo, that engineering marvel which triumphed over the steep heights of La Veta, the road to Conejos, and the Latin civilization of New Mexico and the South, centre here, while the diversion of traffic, due to the opening of the Villa Grove extension, bring closer ties that bind Alamosa to Denver, her great rival on the north. Artesian wells supply the citizens with the bright, white water of their crystal streams, and the glittering incandescence of electric lights on the streets, offices and business houses fringes with its stars "the trailing garments of the night." The amount of trade conducted at Alamosa has an ever increasing volume and the stored treasures of her merchants find fitting homes in the brick buildings, symmetrical, spacious and serviceable, which contain them. Four churches, the offerings of the Episcopalians, Presbyterians, Methodists and Catholics, adorn the city, and point with their admonishing spires to the blue skies of

BANK OF ALAMOSA—INTERIOR VIEW

BIRD'S-EYE VIEW OF ALAMOSA

Colorado. The residence houses, which so charmingly grace the outskirts and suburbs, have much of architectural art, and form luxurious homes with their æsthetically furnished rooms for Alamosa's hospitable families. The historic river of the Rio Grande sweeps or ripples hard by with its murmuring waters, and the planting of trees in parks and pleasure places already begins to give promise of a vigorous growth. The great ditch companies which have reclaimed from nature to the uses of man so many thousand acres of fertile lands, have their offices in Alamosa, and the enquiries received from Eastern intending purchasers for lands in the San Luis Valley, fully occupy the careful time of an army of officials and clerks. The crops raised this fall in the immediate vicinity of Alamosa have surprised even the most enthusiastic believers, and the immense development of agriculture in recent years which has displaced the rough methods of the range and induced the application of scientific farming will, without doubt, be doubled in the fullness of the New Year. From mineral wealth too, Alamosa can claim to draw her share of custom, and Platoro and Sierra Blanca are not unvalued satellites in the calls they make on her merchants. There are two banks in Alamosa, the First National and the Bank of Alamosa, both institutions of considerable prominence in Southern Colorado, while other financiers in various loan and real estate offices are ever ready to afford information, advice or the more solid satisfaction of the highest loans on the easiset terms. The large stocks of goods carried by the Alamosa merchants, owing to her unchallenged possession of the best railroad facilities in the Valley and consequent abatement of uncompromising freights, can be, and are wholesaled and retailed at no exorbitant rates. There is already here a considerable movement in town property and lots. The present main business portion of the town runs the

MANDERS BUILDING

ARTESIAN WELL AT ALAMOSA

whole length of Sixth street, where each store has its plate glass front, its awning and spacious stretch of sidewalk for pedestrians. But the demands of the times are calling for a further extension and the current of trade is steadily blowing in the direction of State avenue, where it is an open secret that ten two story buildings will be built in the spring. Long before the verdant green returns to our grassy fields, Alamosa town lots will be a valuable property and a gilt-edged security, but just now on the edge of December snows and the January frosts, the price at which they are offered is far below the appreciation and attention which Alamosa is obtaining on the outside. Almost daily some new business enterprise is started here and never without a satisfactory return. Our increasing population will find room here and prosper in the bright climate of Colorado. Well may Alamosa deserve her title of the Queen City of San Luis as she grows in beauty under the smiles or snows of her eternal hills, while the whispering wooing of her name is calling to the tiller of the barren fields of New Jersey, the snowy plains of Minnesota, or the malarial swamps of Missouri to leave their cares and troubles at the threshold of the West.

The streets of Alamosa are wide and spacious. There is no over-crowding, no grudging of room, and the class of buildings which are now erected have driven to the confines the shanty of the old happy-go-lucky days. The Masonic Block and Temple on Fifth street is a structure of commanding solidity which has not only large reception rooms, a magnificent lodge room and a brilliant banqueting hall, but also contains the well arranged postoffice, the office of the *Courier* and other rooms, stores and accommodations. There are sixty members here in the Masonic lodge, a number which emphatically endorses the prosperity of the fraternity. Opposite the Masonic Temple the Odd Fellows' Hall,

THE ALAMOSA MILLING AND ELEVATOR COMPANY

a building of the same calibre and architectural design forms the abode and shrine of real estate. Lots on Fifth street promise to become excellent property. Probably the largest edifice on State avenue at present is the Armory Hall which affords a drill room for the popular militia company of Alamosa, glitters with the lights and beauties of the ball room, or affords accommodations to the large audiences of Alamosa on the occasion of a play or opera on its ample and electric-lighted stage.

In these days of railroad extension or rumor new towns are springing up like mushrooms wherever the smoky trail of an engine or the rushing train gives a glimpse of something from a distance, for a moment, to the curious native, the next leaves him forlorn to gaze after the retreating cars and settle down to wait patiently for next day and this one poor amusement in the monotonous sea of routine. There may be money behind these enterprises, but it is money in many instances meant only as a decoy to capture gold dollars for silver and (to use a western metaphor) in roping in by false hopes a deluded population to heel its promoters in a different manner. Alamosa is no mushroom town, no product of a night, no imagination of the fertile brain of the boomer or the paper product of printer's ink. Alamosa's growth has been sterling, steady and substantial. In 1878, just after the trains had begun to thunder down the declivity of Veta Pass to the flowery but now faded city of Garland, and the wide-horned, wild-eyed Texas steer started in surprise at the sight of the engine which brought with it a new civilization and the day of doom for his scraggy anatomy, Governor Hunt, President of the Denver and Rio Grande Construction Company, first laid out Alamosa down here among the *alamo* trees, and for three years Alamosa became the terminus of the road till it was pushed through to Conejos, Champa and Espanola. Alamosa

THE CHICAGO CLOTHING HOUSE
Sol Schwartz, Proprietor

was next chosen as a divisional headquarters and machine shops were erected and other improvements brought about. The branch extended to Monte Vista and Del Norte and the late Villa Grove extension has still further contributed to the centrality of Alamosa. The depot buildings are large, commodious and amply provide for the immense amount of passenger and freight travel daily handled.

Alamosa has long been an incorporated town. The present corporation consists of the following prominent citizens: H. I. Ross, of the First National Bank, mayor; and councilmen C. M. Ball, J. A. McDonald, M. B. Colt, C. L. Miller, M. C. Taylor and Frank Ruby. Their civic cares, in view of the present growth of the city, are no sinecure, and they occupy with dignity and dispatch the honorable place to which they have been called by their fellow townsmen, and the duties it involves. The legal and medical professions are also well represented in Alamosa.

There is an industry which it is hoped will be introduced in the near future. Down south a million sheep crop the sweet grasses of New Mexico, and there is as yet no woolen manufactory in Alamosa to handle the snowy fleeces and make them into the garments of humanity. A woolen mill would be of no inconsiderable benefit to the town, and the raw material should also be forthcoming in the Valley for the manufacture of leather.

MANDERS BUILDING.—The above named building is without doubt the finest in Alamosa. It is located on the corner of San Juan Avenue and Fifth Street, opposite the First National Bank, and was erected during the present year. It is built of white sandstone, is 56 x 80 feet, and is two stories in height. It contains two store-rooms on the ground floor and twenty office-rooms up stairs. Mr. Robert F. Manders is the owner.

SOL. SCHWARTZ.—Among the comparatively new and successful business enter-

THE BALL BLOCK—C. M. BALL, DRUGGIST

prises of the city of Alamosa none stand out more prominently than the Chicago Clothing House, of which Mr. Sol Schwartz is the proprietor, and which was established August 1st, 1891. He occupies a neat and commodious storeroom, and carries a fine line of clothing in every style, while his line of furnishing goods, notions, neckwear, etc. is not easily duplicated.

C. M. BALL.—The leading drug house of the San Luis Valley is the one of which the above named gentleman is proprietor. Mr. Ball established the business in 1880. The salesroom is particularly neat and pleasing in appearance, reminding one more forcibly of a large city drug store than any other house in this section. Here can be found an exceptionally large stock of drugs, medicines, chemicals, proprietary medicines, perfumes, toilet requisites, as well as a most comprehensive stock of paints, oils, glass, etc., and a large assortment of the very best wines and liquors for medicinal purposes. The Ball Block, in which this establishment is located, was finished in September of this year, and is one of the handsomest buildings in the city.

THE ALAMOSA MILLING AND ELEVATOR COMPANY.—The Alamosa Milling and Elevator Company started in business December 1st, 1890. This is the largest and most complete establishment of the kind in the Valley, and has a capacity of 300 barrels per day. They manufacture "Blanca," "Four Ace" and "Mountain Pink" flour, and are wholesale dealers in hay and grain. The sale of its products is widespread, reaching into the neighboring States and Territories; due, of course, to the superior article of flour this institution has placed upon the market. It expends thousands of dollars annually among the farmers of the Valley, and is prepared to handle all their grain. The officers and directors of the company are: J. K. Mullen, President and General Manager; John A. McDonald, Vice President; M. A. Bowen, Secretary; C. H.

INTERIOR VIEW OF J. SPRIESTERSBACH & CO.'S HARDWARE STORE

Wilkins, Treasurer and H. E. Johnson, Resident Manager.

J. SPRIESTERSBACH & CO.—The oldest house in the particular line it represents in the San Luis Valley is that of J. Spriestersbach & Co., successors to the Alamosa Hardware Company, which succeeded Alva Adams & Bro. The "Co." of the firm is the Hon. Alva Adams, Ex-Governor of Colorado, and a gentleman who is one of the best known and most favorably regarded citizens in the State. This firm is not only the oldest in the Valley, but it is also the largest of the kind. They are extensive dealers in shelf and heavy hardware of all kinds, farming implements of the best makes, wagons and buggies, sporting goods of all descriptions, and artesian well supplies. There is nothing in their line that they do not handle. They are also manufacturers of copper, tin and sheet iron ware on an extensive scale.

BANK OF ALAMOSA.—Prominent among the commercial establishments of this city, and one that is ranked as the most substantial agency for providing the community with financial accommodations is the Bank of Alamosa. This bank is a private institution, and is owned by Messrs. Abe and I. W. Schiffer. It was opened for business on July 18th, 1890, under most favorable auspices, and has always been conducted according to the most approved methods of equity and commercial integrity. It does a general banking business, including foreign and domestic exchange, negotiating loans, making collections, etc. Among its correspondents are a number of the most prominent banks in this country. The owners of the bank are ambitious, enterprising men, and are gentlemen of the strictest honor and integrity. They have been residents of the Valley eighteen years, having formerly been engaged in the general merchandise business at Del Norte.

WILBUR & SON.—Among the more prominent firms that of Wilbur & Son

WILBUR & SON'S BLACKSMITH SHOP

deserves special mention by reason of the fact that it is a model and representative establishment. The firm is composed of Messrs. J. M. and F. B. Wilbur. They have lived in the Valley nearly four years, and have been in business a little more than one year. They are blacksmiths and wagon makers and dealers in all kinds of wagon and carriage material. They are thoroughly proficient in their line and control a very extensive patronage, all earned through the excellent class of work they turn away from their establishment.

FIRST NATIONAL BANK.—The First National Bank of Alamosa is the successor to the Bank of San Juan, which was organized in 1876, and has been doing business under its new charter since 1884. The First National's authorized capital is $100,000, of which $50,000 has been paid in. The officers are: H. I. Ross, President; John L. McNeil, Vice-President; Wm. F. Boyd, Cashier and W. H. Mallett, Assistant Cashier. Its officers are men of business penetration and judgment, and the business of the institution is conducted on safe, conservative principles. It is eligibly located, and occupies elegant quarters, with the finest of office equipments. The fire proof vault is very roomy and the safe represents the very best of steel, burglar proof work. It is a bank of deposit, and special attention is given to preserving the accounts of business men. Interest is allowed at a very fair rate on time deposits. Loans are negotiable at reasonable rates, and satisfactory treatment is guaranteed to all customers. Drafts may be had upon all the principal cities, and exchange—foreign and domestic—is bought and sold. It is the aim of the management to afford every possible facility to customers in the transaction of business.

GEORGE A. WILLIS.—The subject of this sketch has been in the real estate, loan and insurance business several years, and has handsomely fitted-up

HELLMAN & SCHIFFER'S BOOK AND STATIONERY STORE—INTERIOR VIEW

rooms in the Masonic block on Fifth street. He is recognized as an authority on the value of property in all parts of the city and Valley, and investors who are guided by his judgment and advice may rely on securing property that will yield a handsome income and rapidly increase in value. He also possesses excellent facilities for the prompt negotiation of loans. In the insurance line he represents a large number of the best and strongest companies doing business in this State. Mr. Willis is also a collection agent, and all business in that line entrusted to him will receive prompt and careful attention. He solicits correspondence, and furnishes the best of references as to his reliability.

HELLMAN & SCHIFFER.—Prominent among the booksellers and stationers of the San Luis Valley is the firm above mentioned, which consists of Messrs. Morris Hellman and David Schiffer, and which succeeded M. V. Gault some four months ago, the length of time Mr. Schiffer has lived in the Valley, while Mr. Hellman has been a resident of the county some seven years. The firm carries the largest stock in its line to be found in the Valley, and which comprises books, periodicals, stationery of all kinds, the finest of confectionery, nuts and fruits as well as a most magnificent assortment of all grades of wall paper, art and fancy goods, notions, etc. Here also may be found a splendid stock of the best brands of cigars, tobaccos, etc. Messrs. Hellman & Schiffer have the exclusive agency for the "San Luis Illustrated," in Alamosa.

JOHN FRANK & BRO.—The establishment conducted by Messrs. John Frank & Bro. had its inception in 1888. Their storeroom presents throughout an attractiveness that never fails to draw the attention of the passer-by, and which on close examination shows a magnificent display of watches, clocks, diamonds, silverware and jewelry in endless variety and kinds. The Messrs. Frank devote

INTERIOR VIEW OF S. SLAVICK'S SALOON, ALAMOSA

their personal attention to the business, thus insuring the most perfect satisfaction to their patrons. This enterprise is well worth the attention of all lovers of the beautiful in art, and is an honor to the city. Mr. Simon Frank is a practical watchmaker and is competent to adjust the most complicated watches that may have gotten out of order. The firm (composed of John and Simon Frank) are also licensed watchmakers to the Denver and Rio Grande. They deal in Navajo and Chama Indian blankets and pottery, and in musical merchandise of different kinds.

S. SLAVICK.—Six years ago the subject of this sketch came to Alamosa, and at once took a place as one of the town's leading and most highly esteemed citizens. Two years ago he opened his place on Sixth street, and it is by far the handsomest resort for gentlemen in this part of the country. The fixtures are gems of art, and cost a large sum. Everything about the house is in perfect keeping, being neat, clean and attractive. Here will be found only the very best brands of wines, liquors and cigars, both imported and domestic. A poor quality of goods cannot be bought in this house, as they are not kept. Slavick's is the most popular resort in Alamosa, due to courteous, liberal treatment, and honorable dealing at all times and under all circumstances.

ALAMOSA CLUB.—By all odds the most artistic building in Alamosa is the Alamosa Club house, which was erected this year. On the first floor there are large and splendidly lighted reading and billiard rooms; also an office. On the second floor are the card room and four sleeping rooms. The rooms are without exception handsomely furnished and are large and commodious. The Alamosa Club is composed of the leading men of the town and is quite a factor in the social life of the Valley.

MASONIC TEMPLE.—This is one of the finest and most substantial buildings in the San Luis Valley, and reflects the

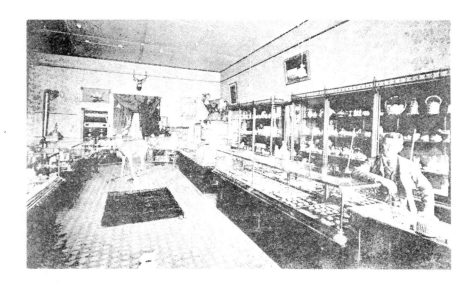

INTERIOR VIEW OF J. FRANK & BRO.'S JEWELRY STORE

greatest credit upon the Masonic fraternity as well as the town of Alamosa, where it is located. The building was erected in 1887. It is 78 x 80 feet, with warehouses in the rear 75 x 40. The splendid storerooms on the ground floor are occupied by a general merchandise store, drug store, and postoffice and hardware store. In the second story there are six office rooms, handsomely furnished, and occupied by the Blue Lodge, Chapter and Commandery.

LA JARA

La Jara is a promising American town situated in the centre of Conejos County, on the Fourth Division of the Denver and Rio Grande Railroad, midway between Alamosa and Antonito, and is surrounded by some of the very best agricultural land in the San Luis Valley. What can be said of the other Valley towns in regard to healthfulness of climate, beautiful location and fertility of soil can be applied to La Jara without the least detraction. All the land west, north and east of town is under cultivation and yielding abundantly in small grain, potatoes and vegetables. Strawberries, blackberries, gooseberries and currants are also raised in this vicinity with success. Experiments are now being made by a number of our progressive farmers with fruit trees of the apple, plumb, cherry and other hardy varieties, which, from present indications, will prove more than an experiment. The country is well supplied with water from the Alamosa and La Jara Rivers for irrigation purposes, and the town is built over a subterranean lake, and water of the purest quality can be struck at from thirty to ninety feet at any place in this vicinity. Contractors will guarantee a flowing artesian well for twenty-five dollars. The temperature of the water from the artesian wells is 48 degrees. Experts claim the water here of the right temperature and the purest and best in

INTERIOR OF M. B. COLT'S OFFICE

BIRD'S-EYE VIEW OF LA JARA

America for brewing purposes. A Denver brewer once made the remark that one of these artesian wells would be worth $100,000 in his business. The supply of water is practically inexhaustible, and although new wells are being continually sunk, the quality and force of flow remains the same. A practical test was made by our farmers in a few instances and proves that irrigation by artesian wells is a grand success in this neighborhood. Four years ago this town contained a railroad water tank and a station house, and Mr. J. W. Hinton, the operator, was the only inhabitant, while to-day we have a large number of cosy residences, stores, two churches,—one Methodist and one Episcopalian,—and a brick school house, with a population of about three hundred. The town is behind the country or the country is ahead of the town. The farms around La Jara, within a radius of ten miles, are sufficient to support a city of 4,000 inhabitants, but this trade is at present diverted from its proper channel and is taken to other towns. A flour mill at this place is absolutely necessary to get the trade of the farmers, and it would be a big paying concern, as some of the best wheat in Conejos County, weighing from sixty to sixty-one pounds to the bushel is raised within a mile of town. Alamosa's best flour is manufactured from wheat raised here. It is really astonishing that such a good point for a flour mill as this is, had not attracted the attention of capitalists long ago. La Jara in its infancy was a lively town and at that time had double its present population, with two town companies and two weekly newspapers to boom it. Its effervescent population is now gone and it has settled down to a solid, permanent basis and is the nucleus of a thrifty, prosperous, agricultural, commercial and manufacturing city. Our merchants, although only a few in number, are all doing a prosperous business. It is also the distributing point for freight

W. A. BRAIDEN'S LIVERY STABLE

for a number of towns off the railroad. Its location is beautiful. Nestling, as it does, in the southern end of the San Luis Valley, a park 120 miles long and 60 miles wide, appearing perfectly level to the eye, and reminding one of an immense billiard table where the fabled giants tossed mountains and left them standing on the very edge where they remain to the present day. Here on their plateau, hemmed in by snow-capped mountains, surrounded by verdant pastures and golden fields of grain within the shadow of Mount Blanca, the sentinel of the rockies, lies La Jara. Can you think of a picture more sublime? Pretty as it is, La Jara is not a place for romance, for Cupid is a stranger here, and love is untold. It was only a few weeks ago that the first wedding was celebrated with all the festivities due such an eventful occasion. Miss Kate Denning, of Conejos, was the bride, and W. G. Eeles, under-sheriff of Conejos County and a resident of La Jara, was the groom. Although a large per cent of its population is made up of single persons of marriageable age, of both sexes, the town was four years old before the first wedding was celebrated. The name La Jara is a Spanish word and signifies "The Willow." It was given this name, perhaps, because there is not a single willow near the town. The buildings of the town, with a few exceptions, are all one story frames. The La Jara drug store occupies the only two story building on Main street, and is the only one in town. The school house is a brick building costing $1,500. The Episcopal church is a frame building and was erected by Rev. Amos Bannister. The M. E. church is also a frame and was built by the Methodist congregation, assisted with liberal donations by nearly every citizen of La Jara, costing about $2,200. At present the business of the town is done by three general merchandise stores, one drug store, two hardware stores, one farming machinery and implement establishment,

WILSON & McCREADY'S GENERAL MERCHANDISE STORE

one livery stable, one real estate office, one saloon, one harness maker and saddlery, one furniture dealer, one lumber and building material dealer, two coal dealers, one barber, one blacksmith, one hotel, one meat market, one painter and paper hanger and three doctors. Probably the main reason why a flour mill and brewery have not been established here is on account of other towns offering inducements to such enterprises, while La Jara holds her natural advantages only, as her baits. The ranches in this vicinity are models of their kind. The horse ranch, a few miles from town, and owned by John Harvey, of Leadville, and managed by his son, John Harvey, Jr., is famed all over the State for its fine horses. D. E. Newcomb, S. E. Newcomb, L. D. Eskridge and David F. How are among the most prosperous farmers in this vicinity. The average yield per acre is as follows: Wheat, 35 bushels; barley, 55 bushels; oats, 75 bushels, and potatoes 18,000 ponnds.

W. A. BRAIDEN.— Mr. Braiden has been in business here some five years, and in that short space of time has built up a business of splendid proportions. He occupies the largest business premises in the town, over 12,000 square feet of floorage, and is a dealer in buggies, wagons and farming implements of the very best manufacture. He carries in stock at all times a number of vehicles and machines of various makes and styles, as well as wagon and carriage material. He also deals in Glidden barb wire, hay presses and threshing machines. Likewise in building material and furniture, and hardwood and eastern lumber. Mr. Braiden also handles hay, grain and the best qualities of coal. In addition to the various lines enumerated above, he is proprietor of the Pioneer Livery Barn, which has an enviable reputation throughout the San Luis Valley for excellent rigs and thorough service. This barn is located in a most central and eligible

J. B. FORBES' GENERAL MERCHANDISE STORE

position, and is large and commodious, being thoroughly ventilated, etc. Here can always be found a large number of handsome rigs and fine driving and riding horses, the stables being in all respects the peer of any in the Valley. Mr. Braiden is one of La Jara's best known and most highly respected citizens. He is a thorough gentleman and one with whom it is a pleasure to transact business.

WILSON & McCREADY.—This firm is composed of Messrs. LeRoy Wilson and J. W. McCready and they established their business on the first of last July. Mr. Wilson has lived in the Valley some four years, while Mr. McCready is comparatively a new comer, his residence dating from June of the present year. Mr. Wilson is one of the pioneers of La Jara, having helped build the first hotel, and also among the first houses in the town. This establishment is one of the best known in the Valley, and carries a large and splendidly assorted stock of that class of goods usually found in first-class establishments of a similar kind, such as gents' furnishing goods, boots and shoes, dry goods, staple and fancy groceries, flour, feed, etc. The gentlemen are large dealers in those commodities, buying in such large quantities that they secure the lowest figures, and give their patrons the benefit of good judgment and the very lowest prices. They are energetic business men and richly deserve the success they have achieved.

J. B. FORBES.—Mr. Forbes carries in stock a complete assortment of everything usually found in a well conducted general merchandise store. The stock carried by Mr. Forbes is so large that we cannot enumerate it. Suffice it to say that his is, in every sense of the word, a complete general merchandise establishment. Personally, Mr. Forbes is a most pleasant gentleman, and he owes his enviable position in the world of trade and credit to the fact that he has always pursued an honest, conservative business policy, never misrepresenting and always

F. G. BLAKE'S HARDWARE AND IMPLEMENT STORE

giving value received for every dollar he has taken in, in the two years that he has done business in La Jara.

F. G. BLAKE.—The gentleman whose name heads this sketch occupies a more conspicuous place in his particular line than any other house in this section of the State. This enviable position has been gained by the honorable and intelligent efforts put forth by Mr. Blake, who is intimately identified with the town, and who has figured prominently in the growth and prosperity of the city. He has lived in the Valley three years and has been in his present business one year. The facilities of his establishment meet the requirements in every particular, and is all that could be expected from a modern American institution of this character. He is an extensive dealer in shelf and heavy hardware, wagons, buggies, farm implements and machinery, stoves, tinware and sporting goods. His business premises are large and commodious, and filled with a large and comprehensive supply of goods in this line. Mr. Blake is a go-ahead, enterprising business man and a good citizen. He is President of the San Luis Valley Town and Investment Company, which was founded in 1888, and in which he owns a controlling interest. This company owns the best property in La Jara, which is offered for sale at most reasonable prices.

A. H. BOLINGER.—This gentleman has lived in Colorado two years, coming from Iowa. He has been in business in La Jara about five months, and has one of the most complete blacksmith and wagon making shops in the San Luis Valley. He has already secured a remunerative trade, which is growing at a most satisfactory rate. Mr. Bolinger bears the well-earned reputation of being one of the best smiths in the Valley, and as he has a thorough knowledge of his business, he turns out absolutely first-class work at all times. He is an honorable, upright gentleman of

A. H. BOLINGER'S BLACKSMITH SHOP

liberal and progressive ideas, and always lends his aid to any legitimate plan for the advancement of his section.

A. D. TUTTLE.—The gentleman whose name heads this short sketch has long been esteemed one of La Jara's most popular citizens and one of the foremost men of the Valley. He located here four years ago and since that time has followed his trade as a saddler and harness maker. Mr. Tuttle is a practical workman and turns out only honest goods; so that he has achieved a magnificent reputation in the commercial world, of which he is an honored member. He carries in stock a complete line of such goods as are usually found in a well equipped and first-class harness and saddlery establishment, including harness of various kinds, all grades of saddles, bridles, whips, spurs, quirts, etc., and also repairs anything in his line in a first-class manner and at the most reasonable prices commensurate with good work. Mr. Tuttle's reputation as the best in his line in this section is unquestioned. He built the first house in La Jara and was first to advance the interests of the town.

W. B. CAMPBELL & CO.— Prominent among the leading and extensive houses in the grocery business is that of W. B. Campbell & Co., which was established in June, 1891, and at all times carries a complete and fresh stock of staple and fancy groceries, queensware, crockery, dry goods, boots and shoes, foreign and domestics fruits, etc. This house enjoys such commercial privileges that it is enabled to offer discounts to the trade throughout the San Luis Valley and the West that cannot be procured from any other house in a similar line. The growth and prosperity of this responsible establishment is only commensurate with the energy and enterprise of its proprietors, Messrs. W. B. Campbell and W. H. Johnson.

DUNLAP & ELLIS.— A neat and elegantly fitted up drug store in this city, and one that enjoys a large share of

A. D. TUTTLE'S HARNESS SHOP

popularity and patronage, is the one conducted by Messrs. W. G. Dunlap and H. O. Ellis. This business was established about two years ago and has ever been conducted according to the strictest principles of equity and business integrity. The house is stocked with a large assortment of pure and fresh drugs, medicines, perfumeries, fancy articles, toilet requisites and a large and comprehensive stock of books and stationery of the best grades. Special attention is given to the prescription department, which is acknowledged to be without a superior in the entire San Luis Valley. Dunlap & Ellis have lived in this valley one and two years respectively and have made a large number of staunch friends. They are progressive, liberal-minded gentlemen, who always do their share towards helping any project for the advancement of this section.

THE HARVEY RANCH

Whatever John Harvey undertakes to do, he does thoroughly. When he first established the great coal and hay business which has won him fortune in Leadville, he recognized the fact that the steep gradients of the streets and the high ascents to the mines necessitated a class of horses which would stand the altitude and draw the heaviest loads up the steepest inclines or through the deepest snows of that exalted region. For this purpose the great Percheron-Norman breed seemed to offer the greatest promise. Their muscle, docility and weight gave the qualifications desired. No inferior animal was ever hitched up to Mr. Harvey's wagons, and the people would stop on the streets of Leadville to admire the magnificent proportions of the steeds which drew to their destinations the immense loads of black diamonds. Mr. Harvey's satisfaction with his experiment was such that he determined to breed his own horses, and after various initial land investments near Leadville, came to the

W. B. CAMPBELL & CO.'S GENERAL MERCHANDISE STORE

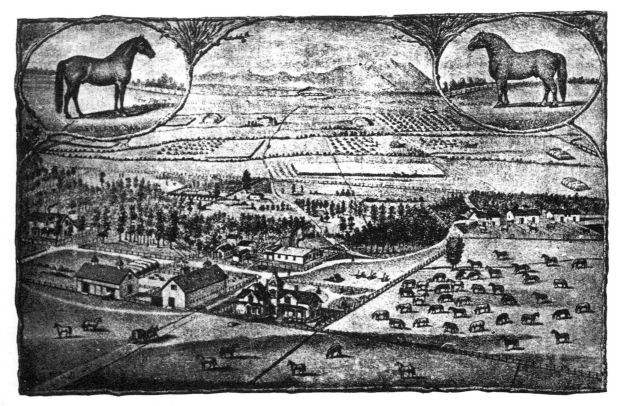

JOHN HARVEY'S HORSE RANCH

conclusion that the San Luis Valley possessed the best land, best climate and best opening for the execution of his plans. Here some three years ago he purchased from L. W. Wainwright one of the finest and best adapted ranches in the fertile neighborhood of La Jara and brought his already large heard of noble Percherons. At the inception of his entry into horse breeding, Mr. Harvey imported thirty head of big brood mares from Canada and added to their numbers from time to time selections from the best blooded stock of Iowa and Illinois. Four hundred head of horses now browse on the rich herbage of his La Jara ranch, managed and operated by John Harvey, Jr., who has grown to a practical experience and judgment in horseflesh which yearly brings the most satisfactory results. At the head of the herd is the veteran imported Percheron Docile, who last year won the first prize and sweepstakes at the Alamosa fair. He pulls down the scales at 1,850 pounds; his progeny inherit the virtues of their sire. The Percheron Victory looms up in his stable with ponderous proportions, weighing 2,110 pounds and is worthily represented by his numerous offspring. Sampson the IX, an imported English Shire stallion is a bay beauty, weighing 1,800 pounds, clean limbed, massive chested, stout and reliable. That fine young Cleveland Bay, the Squire, also a prize winner at Alamosa, adds his attraction to the stud, and Mr. Harvey has already some promising youngsters of his which will some day shine in harness on the road. There were ninety head of colts raised on the ranch this year and their merits ever cause prompt sales. Mr. Harvey's horses are always sound in wind and limb and the closest inspection would declare them without a fault or blemish. Some of the improvements Mr. Harvey has placed on this splendid property may be judged from the accompanying cut of the charming home he has built and the neatly arranged

DUNLAP & ELLIS'S DRUG STORE

barn and stables. The ranch contains 3,400 acres under fence and partition fence. Three hundred and fifty acres seeded to alfalfa returned over three tons to the acre last year, and 300 acres of oats gave the big average yield of thirty-five bushels. In addition to this, native grass under fence gave a crop of 800 tons of hay and there is ample winter feed in the pasture fields. The ranch slopes gently from west to east within three miles of the La Jara railroad station and is watered by Alamosa Creek. Two artesian wells provide water for the stock, and there is no single feature or possible requirement for horse raising that has been overlooked. Under Mr. John Harvey, Jr.'s management, everything on the place responds to his care and supervision, and the Harvey horse farm is distinctly one of the modern ranches of the San Luis Valley.

REEKER & EELES.—These gentlemen are the proprietors of one of the best known and most popular resorts in Conejos County, which is called the Board of Trade. Messrs. Reeker & Eeles carry one of the largest and best selected stocks of foreign and domestic wines, liquors and cigars to be found anywhere in the Valley, and they have attained a most excellent record for honest and square dealing. They have also a splendid billiard and pool parlor, where one may enjoy knocking about the ivories on some of the best tables in the land. The Board of Trade is deservedly popular, and its proprietors are among the most enterprising and successful business men in the San Luis Valley.

CONEJOS

The county-seat of this county is just one mile north-west of Antonito proper, off the railroad. The raging waters of the Conejos River pass to the north of the town, dividing the two towns, or plazas, of Conejos and Guadelupe. The two towns are inhabited principally by

REEKER & EELES' SALOON

Mexicans, although the county officers are all Americans except the Sheriff. The office of Sheriff is ably filled by Hon. Jose A. Garcia, who is just commencing his third term.

The Palace Mills are owned by Ex-Governor Lafayette Head and managed by Charles S. Lawton. A fair quality of flour is manufactured. The mill has a capacity of fifty barrels in twenty-four hours. The Conejos river furnishes the water-power for about nine months in the year; the balance of the year the mill is operated by steam-power.

There is only one general merchandise store in the place.

A $40,000 court house stands in the middle of the public square. It is built of soft lava stone, which polishes nicely. The building is three stories high, with the jail and cells underneath the main structure. The building commands an imposing view from the railroad, which passes to the east of the town one half mile. The architectural design of the outside is beautiful, while the interior is roomy and convenient. This edifice was erected less than two years ago. Previous to the erection of this spacious building

the county officers were habited in old adobe houses.

A large Catholic church and academy is just south of the new court house. The educational department is presided over by the Sisters of Loretto. There are two resident priests, who have charge of several congregations in Conejos County. The Mexican people are mostly all members of this religious denomination. On special occasions 2,000 to 3,000 of these worshipers meet at this church to enjoy their religious rites; they come from far and near. Ex-Governor Lafayette Head was perhaps the first white man to settle in this part of the San Luis Valley. It was after the war with Mexico; he was returning home when he was delighted with this portion of the country and concluded to locate here. That was more than forty years ago and he has continued to live here ever since. The Apache Indians had full possession of the country at that time. He brought with him a colony of Mexicans, and they first encamped on the north bank of the Conejos River, now Guadeloupe. Many of these hardy pioneers are still living. They had many

narrow escapes from the savages, and many were murdered. A fort was built and Major Head was the leader in defending the settlers from the depredations of the bloodthirsty Apaches. The early settlers underwent many hardships and privations before they were able to raise anything to subsist upon. There was plenty of wild game, which was a godsend to the new settlers, or there would have been more suffering than there was. Among the first colonists who accompanied Major Head to this new land, and who are alive to-day and in the enjoyment of good health and plenty, we will mention Hon. Jose Victor Garcia, father of our present sheriff; Jesus Maria Valdez, ex-sheriff; Juan F. Chacon, Simon Garcia, Jose B. Romero, Commissioner of the insane asylum, and his brother, Hon. Bernardo Romero, the present County Commissioner of this district; a large family of the Lobatos and Valdez, and many others whose names we are unable to recall at this time. Mr. Head is sixty-four or five years of age, hale and hearty. He was the first Lieutenant Governor elected in the State. He has held many positions of honor and

and trust, National, State and county. He has great faith in the future possibilities of the San Luis Valley. He has made many attempts to change his residence but always returns to the Valley with a full determination of passing the remainder of his days where he had spent the best part of his life. Among the prospective enterprises for the development of the country south of Antonito, is a large canal taken from the Conejos and San Antonio Rivers, which will traverse sixty miles into New Mexico, covering an area of over half a million of acres of rich, wild land. The Taos Valley Canal Company have already expended over $50,000 in this enterprise. The intention is to husband the surplus water in the spring of the year by building large reservoirs along the line of this large canal, which can be drawn off and used by the farmers in maturing their crops. This new territory, when opened for the settlers, will grow all kinds of grain, vegetables and fruits, the latter especially. The climate is salubrious, being temperate both winter and summer. It will require perhaps a hundred thousand dollars to complete this canal, which, when finished, will open up a large productive country to the home seeker. The land is subject to homestead and tree culture entry.

ANTONITO

This beautiful and picturesque town is nestled at the mouth of the Conejos Canon, among the pines and cedars of the adjacent foot-hills and mountains. The mountain scenery to the west, south and east is grand. The Denver and Rio Grande Railroad passes through the centre of the town, passing west to Durango and Silverton. Also the Santa Fe Northern taps a branch of this same road at Espanola, New Mexico, which branches off the main line at Antonito to that point, making Antonito a junction of the two roads. This is the principal shipping point for wool, hides and pelts in this portion of the Valley. As this is headquarters for the principal dealers and buyers in southern Colorado, more than half a million dollars in wool alone is shipped annually from this point. The markets of New Mexico are supplied with hay, oats and potatoes that are grown in this vicinity. The town proper contains about four hundred inhabitants, consisting of railroad men, business men and laborers. There are two blacksmith shops, one large furniture store, three large general merchandise establishments, one bakery and confectionery, one drug store, kept by the post-master, one hardware store, one newspaper— *The Sentinel-Echo*, published by Lewis and Seigmund, which is an eight-column weekly and one of the very best newspapers in the Valley; two barber shops and two saloons, two hotels and one livery and feed stable. All business and trades are well represented by men of push. The two rivers, San Antonio, which runs south of Antonito half a mile, and the Conejos River, one mile north of the town, furnish plenty of water to the farmers along the streams for irrigation and plenty to spare. The soil is very productive and everything can be grown here (except corn) that is raised in lower altitudes. The old-time ranchmen are well-to-do, with good improvements and plenty of stock of all kinds. They are prosperous and contented, more so, perhaps, than in other localities. The near mountains and foot-hills furnish the best of summer pasturage, as well as fuel, fencing and building material, which costs nothing but the trouble of hauling it; a fine quality of building stone is found within seven miles of town which is soft when first uncovered but hardens as it is exposed to the elements. This stone can be cut in any shape, with a polished surface. Mr. J. J. Corlett is erecting a business house out of it on Main street, 35x120 feet, polished front. All that is needed to work this rock is an adz to hew with.

The Denver and Rio Grande Railroad has a fine stone depot built of black hard lava rock, and is said to be the most comfortable of any between this point and Pueblo. The company have also a round-house. Antonito was incorporated two years ago, and is a mile square, reaching to the town limits of Conejos on the north. A beautiful and level plateau of vacant land, consisting of less than 100 acres, is all that separates the two towns.

RIO GRANDE COUNTY

MUCH has been said and written in praise of the San Luis Valley, the largest in the great Rocky Mountain range. What first attracts the attention of the stranger is its bracing and healthful atmosphere, its pure streams and perpetual sunshine.

Rio Grande County, lying on the west and reaching into the foot-hills, was one of the first counties to be settled. Here the early prospectors and stock raisers made their homes and their fortunes. Long before irrigation was thought of, it was discovered that the grasses which covered this vast arid plain were very nutritious, and upon which stock thrived exceedingly well both in summer and winter; consequently, it was but a few years before large herds were seen grazing in every direction. Along the streams and creeks a great amount of hay was cut, and before the railroad reached Leadville it received a large part of its hay supply from this Valley. At Del Norte, the seat of Rio Grande County, was commenced the experiment of irrigation. Here the first great canals were started which have demonstrated the fact that nearly the whole Valley is susceptible of irrigation, and, with water, produces the most bountiful and never failing crops of grain and vegetables that can be grown anywhere in the country. This county, which was once devoted entirely to stock raising, is now occupied by farmers who depend more upon their crops of grain, hay and vegetables for shipment than stock growing. At Monte Vista, the Travelers Insurance Company, of Hartford, Conn., have established headquarters for the development and sale of large tracts of land which it came into possession of by expending large sums of money in canal building. This company has opened up the "North Farm," which consists of 2,000 acres, the "South Farm" of 800 acres, and the "East Farm," the "La Garita Farm," and the "Central Farm" of several thousand acres each. The expenditure and disbursements of the Travelers at this place has been one of the means of building up this thrifty and prosperous town, which is claimed by its inhabitants to be the best in the Valley. It is here the Soldiers' Home and Experimental Farm are located, and where health seekers are wont to locate.

Monte Vista is not only one of the best farming towns in the Valley, but it is also becoming one of the best shipping points for the great Summitville and Platoro mines.

This town supports two newspapers, the *Journal* and *Graphic*, both of which are well edited and have a large circulation.

There never was a better or more opportune time for home seekers to settle in the San Luis Valley than at present. The question of water supply need no longer deter anyone. The canals and artesian wells are ample for all purposes. It has been proven that after the land has been once thoroughly wet, but very little water is required for crops.

The wonderful development of Creede camp, with a prospect of its becoming one of the greatest camps in the State, the great bodies of rich ore known to exist at Summitville, Platoro, Jasper, the rich claims near Saguache, and the inexhaustable mines of iron and coke near Villa Grove, insure good markets in the near future for the produce of the farm where crops never fail. There are abundant opportunities for men of small means to secure homes and become independent.

To home seekers and business men Rio Grande County extends a cordial greeting.

MONTE VISTA

As an example of what the great San Luis Valley will justify when taken advantage of by energetic, go-ahead men, the thriving town of Monte Vista commends itself to the attention of all who come within the charmed circle of the mountain belted plain, on pleasure or business intent. The name itself, signifying Mountain View, gives an idea of the natural location and beauties of the town. Situated as it is about fifteen miles west of Alamosa and some nine or ten miles from the western foothills of the Valley, its position is at once both charming and commanding. It is about a mile from the Rio Grande River, and so placed as to give a wide and comprehensive view of plains and mountains

STATE BANK

BIRD'S EYE VIEW OF MONTE VISTA

in every direction. To one standing in the streets of Monte Vista the surface of the landscape seems to sink away in all directions, though as a matter of fact it has a general slope, the same as other portions of the country. The town is well located for drainage purposes, and its streets would seem never to need a paving stone, so admirable is the nature of the soil for the avoidance of mud and slush, in wet weather. As before remarked, the growth of this town may well stimulate and encourage other localities to increase their prosperity and population in the near future. Eight years ago hardly a house stood upon the site where now is a busy, substantial, business town of over a thousand people, which number is steadily increasing from month to month. It was in March, 1884, that the town was first laid out, and during that year only temporary structures were erected in the place, some ten or a dozen of them. Messrs. H. H. Marsh, M. N. Pelton, T. J. Hoyt and Charles Fasset were among the first permanent residents of the town, and that their faith was well fixed is now broadly apparent to all. The site is well watered by the Rio Grande and Lariat canals, which carry water all through the place in abundance, the main ditches being the size of many a California river, and carrying a greater volume of water. The increase in value of these water privileges may be well exemplified from the fact that a share of stock now selling for $50 was worth three years ago only $10. The place now has something over a thousand inhabitants and a number of fine, substantial public and private buildings; especially so, considering the years of its growth. The pride of the town is a large two-story and basement brick school building, with three departments, conducted in an able manner. There is also a large flouring mill, town hall, several good brick and frame blocks, besides numerous smaller store buildings

HOUSE OF H. H. MARSH

and shops. Monte Vista can probably boast of more fine private residences for its size and age than any other town in the Valley, among them being those of Messrs. Aldrich, Powell, Bonner, and several owned by Mr. H. H. Marsh. Many of the streets, all of which are wide and straight, have shade trees planted along their sides, and are provided with sidewalks.

The present condition of Monte Vista shows the result of seven years. The assessed valuation has doubled every year, and still the town is growing and doing a thriving business in nearly all branches. Several new buildings have been put up the present spring, others are building, and still others are contemplated and sure to be erected soon. Lumber may be had in the mountains fourteen miles distant at $12 and $14 per 1,000. A large brick yard near town furnishes plenty of this building material, while six or eight miles away are quarries of fine pink and green lava rock, which make splendid structures. It is easily worked, and when in a block or residence presents a substantial and beautiful appearance. This stone can be used as cheaply as brick, and is practically inexhaustible.

Fuel is now shipped in at a cost of $5 to $7 per ton for coal and $3 to $5 per cord for wood. But there is no doubt that coal exists much nearer to the town than it is now mined, and will yet be much cheaper. Fine water is reached by wells at fifteen to thirty feet, and artesian water will be found, as it has been near the place, and a well has been put down for the town supply on the public street. Monte Vista is a very temperate town. In fact it is a prohibition town. A clause in every deed prohibits the sale of liquor, and an ordinance prohibits its sale nearer than one mile from the limits. As a result the nearest saloon is fifteen miles away, and the people are thrifty and prosperous. However, as the town is growing, there will be a demand for increased business facilities. Reference has been made to the town itself heretofore, and many will ask: What is there to build such a place, to keep it up and cause its increase in future? It is very true that no town can have permanency and prosperity except the country around it furnish resources for its existence, life and progress. The most solid support, too, is agricultural in character. Mining may "play out;" manufacturing may

be overdone, but people must eat and drink, and so long as this is true the agricultural section fills the demand. In this respect Monte Vista is solid. With the start it now has, located fifteen miles from any other town of importance, surrounded by so rich a country, and with so intelligent and enterprising a class of citizens, it is bound to thrive. For twenty miles to the north, twenty miles to the south, as far east and west as it can successfully compete with sister towns, is tributary to it some of the richest agricultural lands in the Valley. The soil is rich alluvial, admirably suited to grains, hay, potatoes and all kinds of vegetables. Water is plentiful, easily utilized and cheap. But a very small portion of the land tributary to Monte Vista is yet cultivated, but even this production has demonstrated what can and will be done in the future.

The two large farms near Monte Vista — the one on the north and the other on the south side of the Rio Grande River—take the lead in grains, both in acreage and yield. The North Farm produced 19,861 bushels of oats, and 18,819 bushels of wheat. The South Farm produced 14,152 bushels of oats, 4,417 bushels of wheat and 1,118 of barley. All the crop fully matured, and the quality of the grain was remarkably good and the yield heavy. The harvest commenced the last week in August, and the best judges put the average yield of wheat at 35 bushels, oats at 55 bushels and barley at 45 bushels. Single acres, picked from the best of these crops, will nearly double these amounts. We cite the following instances: The heaviest crop of oats reported is from Charles Fassett, which was 85 bushels to the acre. The heaviest crop of wheat was raised by Mr. Schott, averaging 40 bushels to the acre. Mr. R. C. Nisbet says he raises almost every year on his farm 30 bushels of wheat, 80 bushels of oats, 60 bushels of barley and 335 bushels of potatoes per acre. He gives the following as the cost and profit of raising grain in the San Luis Valley: The cost of raising an acre of wheat under ordinary circumstances is about as follows: Plowing, $2.50; seed, $1.40 to $1.50 per one hundred pounds; sowing or drilling, 50 cents; making ditch, 50 cents; irrigating, $2.50; harvesting, $1.50; threshing, $1.00 — making a total of $10.00. An average crop is 25 bushels to the acre, of 60 pounds per bushel, at $1.25 per hundred, makes $18.20, or a net profit of $8.20 per acre, exclusive of the straw, which is of considerable value to the farmer in the way of feed and for manuring purposes. The cost applied to oats or barley: An average crop of oats is 35 bushels, of 40 pounds, to the acre, at $1.25 per hundred pounds, leaves a profit of $8.00 per acre. An average crop of barley is 45 bushels to the acre, 50 pounds to the bushel, a net profit of $12.00 per acre. About 150 farmers raised excellent crops for the year 1891, some as high as 3000 bushels, while one-half at least of this number averaged 1000 bushels of grain. In almost every instance the grain overran the regular bushel in weight from 10 to 20 per cent, while the quality of the wheat grown is pronounced by expert millers to

BONNER MEAD BLOCK

be equal to any raised in the United States.

The tendency of a single grain of seed to throw out a large number of healthy and vigorous stalks, each bearing a head of fully matured grain, is one of the wonders of this wonderful Valley. The cause lies in the soil, which is rich in the elements of plant growth, the core springs which hold back top growth and force root development, and in the application of water in just the right quantities at just the right time. Winter wheat develops this tendency in a remarkable degree. A single stool of wheat from the North Farm has shown 175 perfect stalks. It is not uncommon in the grain fields to see stools of wheat, oats and barley with 100 stalks, while stools containing over 200 are frequently found. The number of grains in some of the heads which grow on these ranches reach as high as 115 and seldom fall below 50; assuming 70 to be a fair average, 200 stalks will produce 14,000 grains from a single grain of seed. It is not claimed that this marvelous yield is attained in one field, but the exceptional production growing in favored spots and under favorable conditions, is a constant incentive to the ambitious farmer to bring his average crop up toward the high standard which nature every fall proclaims, by her practical object lessons, to be possible. The annual cost of water from the irrigating canals taken from the Rio Grande River and conveyed over the land is $1 per acre. Wheat, rye and oats yield 20 to 40 bushels per acre; barley 30 to 90; peas 30 to 50; potatoes 100 to 400. All hardy vegetables do well, and native hay yields from one to three tons per acre. Hops are a natural product and yield abundantly. The Denver and Rio Grande Railroad traverses the Valley, and opens the way for its produce to the markets of the State. In several parts of this section there is an abundance of excellent coal. A number of extensive irrigating canals have been constructed and carry sufficient water for all who may desire to enter upon the pursuit of agriculture.

These grains are of the very finest quality. The flour made at the Monte Vista mills took first premium at the exposition in Denver, last fall, over all the State. The town has now only one railroad, but a company has been incorporated to build a line from La Jara, via

WEISS-CHAPMAN DRUG CO.'S STORE

Monte Vista and Saguache, to Villa Grove. A company also proposes to build a road from Pueblo, via Monte Vista, to Durango. It is certain that a road will be run through the Valley sooner or later from Villa Grove south, and Monte Vista builds large hopes that these two roads will yet make her a railroad center.

This was written in July, 1891, since which time its growth has been much greater then ever.

The climate of Monte Vista is the climate of the Valley, and taking it the year through would be hard to improve upon. With all her advantages Monte Vista has undoubtedly a bright and promising future for home seekers and investors in this beautiful Valley.

M. MEAD & SON.—The oldest establishment of the kind in the city is that conducted by Messrs. Marvin Mead and his son Evin E. Mead. Under their proprietorship and management it gives employment to many skilled hands and turns out every style of work demanded by the trade, besides they carry a full and complete line of the best makes in wagons and buggies, all kinds of farm implements, and wagon and carriage material, also coal, iron and barbed wire, and make a specialty of fine repairing in both the blacksmithing and woodworking department. Horse-shoeing is also done by most competent mechanics. This establishment is over seven years old. Mr. Marvin Mead is one of the owners of the Bonner-Mead block, built the first brick house in Monte Vista, and has been a Justice of the Peace in the town for six years.

H. H. MARSH. The gentleman whose name heads this article is the pioneer of Monte Vista. He was the first man to locate in the town, coming from Oakland, Cala., in 1881. Mr. Marsh is one of the largest property owners in the

M. MEAD & SON'S WAGON AND IMPLEMENT ESTABLISHMENT

town, and has done a great deal toward making Monte Vista what she is to-day—the Queen of the Valley.

E. F. HUBBARD.—The meat market of which Mr. E. F. Hubbard is the owner has been established in Monte Vista some six years, and has been under Mr. Hubbard's proprietorship about six months. He occupies a large and well equipped salesroom, heavily stocked with beef, pork, mutton, veal, salt meats of all kinds, game, fish, oysters, vegetables, fruits, etc. His stock is an exceptionally large and select one, and he is fully prepared to meet the demands of both wholesale and retail trade. His refrigerator accommodations for stock are very roomy, and the entire stock is preserved sweet and fresh in even the warmest weather. Mr. Hubbard does a rushing business, which is constantly and steadily growing at a most satisfactory rate. His market is always clean and wholesome and in every particular attractive. In the wholesale line Mr. Hubbard disposes annually of over 4,000 sheep, besides hundreds of head of cattle.

STATE BANK.—The history of the development of Monte Vista as a financial center, has no more interesting chapter than the description of the rise and progress of her banking interests. The State Bank of Monte Vista occupies one of the nicest banking quarters in the San Luis Valley; it was built expressly for them and is a model in arrangement. The great central feature of the financial history of this city is the honored State Bank. After fifteen months of existence this corporation stands to-day more vigorous than ever, the exponent attending the observance of the great cardinal laws of banking and finance. The State Bank of Monte Vista was the outcome of the legitimate wants of the merchants of this city for banking facilities, and has ever been conducted upon an enterprising and yet conservative basis. This bank is incorporated under the State laws, with a capital of $80,000, (the largest

RESIDENCE OF H. H. MARSH

establishment. The stock carried embraces almost everything known in the lines of shelf and heavy hardware, wagons and farm implements, and tents and mining supplies. The firm is composed of Wesley Clark, L. H. Hammond and John Pickett, who established the business over four years ago, and it has been constantly on the increase. Mr. Pickett is the resident partner, and the management of this house falls largely upon his shoulders. The success which this house has attained is due in no small degree to his untiring efforts.

B. F. STEVENS.—The leading establishment of the kind in the San Luis Valley is the large saddlery and harness shop of Mr. B. F. Stevens, who has been actively engaged in the business some thirteen years, formerly living in Scotia, Neb.,

C. C. KERR
Of Kerr & Von Egidy, Real Estate Brokers

capital of any bank in the Valley) with a surplus of over $1,600. The officers are: J. D. Maben, President; L. B. Farrer, Vice-President, and E. M. Perdew, Cashier.

CLARK, HAMMOND & CO.—In writing of Monte Vista and her rapid growth, it becomes a necessity for us to mention the Clark, Hammond & Co., Hardware

INTERIOR VIEW OF CLARK, HAMMOND & CO.'S HARDWARE STORE

HOTEL BLANCA
Owned by The Hartford Loan and Trust Company

There is nothing in the line of horse furnishing goods that this establishment cannot supply. He carries in stock fifty to sixty sets of harness, thirty to forty saddles and other goods in proportion. Prompt and careful attention is given to repairs, and first-class work at moderate prices is assured to patrons.

KERR & VON EGIDY.—In strolling over the city to take in the sights and gather some ideas concerning the business interests of the city generally, we dropped into the office of the well known real estate firm of Messrs. Kerr & Von Egidy, in the Bonner block, to get some pointers on realty values and outlooks. The company is composed of C. C. Kerr and A. R. Von Egidy, gentleman of fine business ability, and they are not slow in showing up the advantages of the locations and

A. R. VON EGIDY
Of Kerr & Von Egidy, Real Estate Brokers

and also in Fairbank, Iowa. From the latter place Mr. Stevens removed to Monte Vista and has lived here five years. He occupies a handsome storeroom and has a perfectly equipped shop. The store room is crowded from end to end and from floor to ceiling with the finest buggy and carriage harness, as well as the most durable of team harness, suitable for ranch and other heavy work.

INTERIOR VIEW OF B. F. STEVENS' HARDWARE STORE

properties they represent. This business affords quite a field for the development and exercise of talent, tact and perseverance, and these gentlemen are taking advantage of the opportunity, and by these, with fair, honest dealings, they are building up quite a flourishing business. The Abstract, Loan and Land Agency is now quite a factor in financial affairs. Many are the times when a little money in hand may be used so as to be more available than double the amount at a future date, and men in this country are cognizant of the fact, and when there is a "snap" to be picked up, they want to see the loan agents and secure the wherewith necessary to attain the end in view, and these gentlemen are always ready to supply any needed help in this direction. By the success they have

L. H. CHENEY
Farm Loan and Insurance Agent

acquired for themselves in the three years they have been established here, they are enabled to lead others to success.

D. J. ELLIOTT.—A leading enterprise in this city and one that adds largely to the manufacturing interests of Monte Vista is the foundry and machine shops of Mr. D. J. Elliott. This gentleman established his business here about three years ago and has already secured a large

D. J. ELLIOTT'S MACHINE SHOP

C. S. CONANT
Editor Monte Vista Journal.

foundry work, it makes this establishment one of importance to the residents of the San Luis Valley.

JACOB LOY, JR.—The premises occupied by Mr. Jacob Loy, Jr., are located very centrally, and are specially fitted up for the drug business, being very commodious and having a neat and attractive appearance. Mr. Loy carries in stock an extraordinarily complete and pure assortment of drugs and chemicals, including compounds, elixirs, druggists' sundries, also fancy goods, toilet requisites, proprietary medicines, etc., his stock being one of the most complete in this section of the State. In addition, Mr. Loy is an extensive dealer in stationery and periodicals. He has been in Monte Vista since 1887.

L. L. FASSETT.—A pioneer house and lucrative trade, being the only establishment of the kind in the city. He manufactures and repairs all kinds of iron and machinery such as could possibly be required in this fast growing community, also doing plumbing of all kinds, and as he carries a complete stock of this class of goods and has the best facilities for all kinds of machinery and

INTERIOR VIEW OF L. L. FASSETT'S GENERAL MERCHANDISE STORE

which continues to be the leading establishment of the kind in the present modern city of Monte Vista, is the general merchandise establishment of Mr. L. L. Fassett, which opened its doors for public patronage over eleven years ago. At that time, goods of all kinds were received from the lumbering van of the freighter, which wound around the stony trails of the mountains to this oasis of the West. But that establishment has undergone changes leading up to its present state of representative perfection, and its progress in all directions has been in keeping with the demands of trade, until to-day the stock carried represents a most comprehensive assortment of dry goods, staple and fancy groceries, provisions, clothing, boots and shoes, hats and caps, furnishing goods, queensware, glassware, etc., etc.

L. D. TROUTFETTER.—The leading jewelry establishment of Monte Vista is that of Mr. L. D. Troutfetter, which was opened for business some three years ago. He is a practical business man of wide experience, and occupies elegant quarters, with a splendid line of watches, clocks, jewelry, diamonds and precious stones, silverware and optical goods. He carries also a fine line of stationery and wall paper, which for quality and prices he guarantees unexcelled in the entire San Luis Valley. Fine watch repairing is a specialty and is promptly attended to, and all work is guaranteed satisfactory. Mr. Troutfetter is an honest man of business and carries an honest line of goods. His recommendation is worthy of consideration in the purchase of goods, and his guarantee means something.

WEISS-CHAPMAN DRUG CO.—One of the leading drug stores in the San Luis Valley and the representative one in Monte Vista, is the one above named, which carries a neat and complete line of drugs and pharmaceutical goods of every nature, embracing all kinds of proprietary and

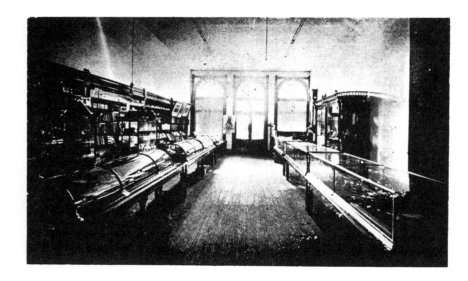

INTERIOR VIEW OF L. D. TROUTFETTER'S JEWELRY STORE

patent medicines, chemicals, etc. Also is carried in conjunction a full assortment and comprehensive stock of watches, clocks, jewelry and diamonds, wall paper, stationery, paints, oils, etc., and marked at prices that prove most satisfactory, as the large trade commanded attests. The firm is composed of Dr. Louis Weiss, who has lived in the Valley eighteen years; Dr. N. H. Chapman, who has been a resident of the San Luis Valley fourteen years, and Mr. Fredrich A. Weiss. The company has branches at Summitville, Del Norte and Creede, and was incorporated in 1887.

L. H. CHENEY.—The gentleman whose name appears at the head of this sketch is one of Monte Vista's oldest and best known citizens, and, in fact, is one of the earliest residents of the town. If our publication reached only the hands of the San Luis Valley people, it would recall to them nothing new when we state that the Colorado Securities Company, which Mr. Cheney represents, is one of the State's best institutions. Those who live here know this to be a fact, and that it is one of the most successful operators in Colorado in both of their specialties. Mr. Cheney, who is the representative of this company in the Valley, has long since established a reputation for honesty and probity second to none. He is thoroughly posted as to property values and can always be relied upon to treat his clients in a strictly honorable and courteous manner. Representing, as he does, one of the best loan institutions in the State, he naturally secures the cream of the business in his line, and it should be said that his personal popularity must also be given credit for a due share of the success he has achieved. He also represents some of the largest and best insurance companies in the country, and gets his share of the business. Mr. Cheney is a wide-awake, progressive business man, who can always be depended upon to do his full share towards advancing the material interests of Monte Vista in particular, and the San Luis Valley in general.

HOTEL BLANCA.—Hotel Blanca was erected during 1888 and 1889, and was opened for business in August, 1889. It is three stories high, the lower story being occupied by offices and stores. It has 45 guest rooms. The main building is 36x132 feet with two L's, one 18x33, the other 46x46. It is lighted by elec-

JACOB LOY, JR.'S DRUG STORE

tricity and heated with steam, and is one of the finest hotels in the State. It is owned by the Hartford Loan and Trust Company. The local offices of the Colorado Valley Land Company, Rio Grande Land and Canal Company, Monte Vista Town and Land Company, are all in Hotel Blanca.

James A. Kelly & Co., are the local agents for the two last named companies.

The Rio Grande Land and Canal Company.
The Monte Vista Canal Company.
The Colorado Valley Land Company.

F. C. Goudy, General Manager, Denver, Colo.
Jas. A. Kelly & Co., General Agents, Land Department, Monte Vista, Colo.

The above named companies were the pioneers in ditch building in the San Luis Valley, and their two canals, The Rio Grande and The Monte Vista, are the largest in the Valley, if not in the State. Perhaps greater credit is due these companies for the settlement and development of the San Luis Valley than to all other influences combined. They have expended immense sums of money in building and developing their canal systems, and in improving their lands. But for their energy and courage in this direction, it is safe to say that a large part of San Luis Valley, where now are hundreds of well cultivated farms and prosperous farmers, would still be occupied as stock ranges—the only use it was formerly supposed which could be made of it. Their policy towards settlers has been eminently liberal and just, and as a result they command the confidence of the people.

Monte Vista is the headquarters of these companies. The Rio Grande Canal is taken from the Rio Grande River, fifteen miles above Monte Vista, and extends north-east thirty-five miles.

C. C. KERR'S RANCH

It is about sixty feet wide on the bottom and ninety feet on top, and carries six feet of water.

The Monte Vista Canal takes its water from the Rio Grande River, about seven miles above Monte Vista, and extends south-east forty-two miles. It is about forty feet wide on the bottom, eighty feet on top, and carries five feet of water.

These two canals together, will water between 200,000 and 300,000 acres of land. Their system of laterals already aggregates about 500 miles.

The lands belonging to these companies, about 80,000 acres, are among the very finest in the Valley. They were originally State lands, and were selected by agents of the State when there were all the lands of the Valley to select from, and they seem to have obtained the cream of the Valley.

The Colorado Valley Land Company have improved many thousands of acres of these lands, as shown by the following list of farms:

North Farm, ... 7,640 acres
South Farm, ... 3,000 acres
East Farm, ... 1,600 acres
Cottage D. Farm, . . . 600 acres
Cottage B. Farm, . . . 215 acres
Central Farm, ... 2,560 acres
La Garita Farm, . . . 2,000 acres
Meadow Farm, ... 6,060 acres

A WONDERFUL SIGHT

All of the above farms are in a high state of cultivation, and present a wonderful sight during harvest time. Their crops of wheat, oats and barley are something to astonish one who is not accustomed to the great crops raised in this Valley.

The Colorado Valley Land Company have not only been very successful themselves in farming, but their manner of preparing their land for market insures the success of the new-comer. It is found that new land broken in the spring will not, in most cases, produce good crops the same year. It should lie over until the next spring before being seeded. But as most purchasers cannot afford to wait a year before beginning to farm, this company, to meet the situation, thoroughly irrigate and then break up thousands of acres of new land every spring and summer. On land thus prepared, the new settler is certain of success from the beginning, and in many cases the first crop will pay for the land.

The wisdom of this policy is well shown in the photographs of harvest scenes reproduced below. The crops illustrated were all grown on new land which had been prepared by the company as above described, and were raised by new settlers from Eastern States who were inexperienced in irrigation.

HARVEST SCENE ON THE RANCH OF D. W. McNUTT

HARVEST SCENE ON THE RANCH OF D. W. McNUTT

AFFIDAVIT OF D. W. McNUTT

Monte Vista, Colo., Dec. 11, '91.

I hereby certify that the two foregoing cuts represent the crop grown on my land this year. I purchased this land, 160 acres (a part of East Farm), of the Colorado Valley Land Company about a year ago for $20 an acre. The land was fenced and plowed. I sowed 93 acres in wheat, which yielded 3,000 bushels; 55 acres in oats, which yielded 2,127 bushels.

D. W. McNutt.

At present prices of grain (wheat $1.12 per hundred weight, oats 90 cents) it will be seen that Mr. McNutt's crop of wheat and oats is worth more than he paid for the land (148 acres) on which it grew.

THE SAN LUIS VALLEY

HARVEST SCENE ON THE RANCH OF A. G. RHOADES

HARVEST SCENE ON THE RANCH OF A. G. RHOADES

AFFIDAVIT OF A. G. RHOADES

MONTE VISTA, COLO., Dec. 21, '91.

This certifies that the two foregoing views are from photographs of the crop on my farm. I purchased this land, 320 acres (a part of East Farm), of the Colorado Valley Land Company, in the fall of 1890, paying therefor $20 an acre. The land was fenced and broken. It was farmed this year by M. H. Anson and son, of Dakota, who did nearly all the work of farming themselves, hiring only one man twelve days while irrigating. They had had no previous experience in farming by irrigation; 150 acres was sown to wheat, 120 in oats, 7 in barley, 1 in peas, 3 in rye, 20 in alfalfa, and 1 planted in potatoes. The peas and rye were sown for pasture and hay. Two cows were pastured all spring and summer on the rye, and it was then mowed three times and yielded about six tons of fine hay. The acre of peas yielded four tons of excellent hay. I have just begun threshing, therefore can give only an estimate of the yield of grain. Judging by the crops threshed by my neighbors, and from the yield at the machine, my wheat will average at least thirty-five bushels per acre, and the oats about fifty bushels, and the barley about forty bushels per acre.

I would not sell this farm for $50 an acre.   A. G. RHOADES,

1919 Grant Avenue,

Denver, Colo.

The value of Mr. Rhoades' whole crop is certainly worth all he paid for the farm.

HARVEST SCENE ON THE RANCH OF JOHN KRAMER

AFFIDAVIT OF JOHN KRAMER

MONTE VISTA, COLO., Dec. 21, '91.

I hereby certify that the foregoing cut is from a photograph of the crop on my farm. I purchased this farm, 160 acres, of the Colorado Valley Land Company, in the fall of 1890, paying therefor $20 an acre. The land was fenced and broken. I seeded 118 acres in wheat, and about 30 acres in oats. My wheat yielded 3,839 bushels, or 32½ bushels per acre. Many acres of it yielded over 50 bushels per acre. I entrusted the irrigation of the oats to an incompetent irrigator with the result that I obtained a poor yield of oats, getting only 700 bushels. Still, at present prices of grain, my whole crop is worth more than the land on which it grew, at $20 an acre.

JOHN KRAMER.

HARVEST SCENE ON THE RANCH OF J. B. F. GEORGE

HARVEST SCENE ON THE RANCH OF J. B. F. GEORGE

AFFIDAVIT OF J. B. F. GEORGE

MONTE VISTA, COLO., Dec. 18, '91.

I hereby certify that the two foregoing cuts are from photographs of the crop on my farm. I purchased 80 acres of this land of the Colorado Valley Land Company, in the fall of 1890, for $19 an acre, broken but not fenced. I leased the other 80 of the same company. On the 160 acres, 100 acres had been broken during the summer of 1890. The yield of various crops was as follows: 47 acres of wheat yielded 2,284 measured bushels.

This wheat tested 61½ pounds per bushel, making an average yield by weight of 49 and four-fifths bushels per acre: 35 acres of oats yielded 2,780 measured bushels. This oats tested 45 pounds per measured bushel, making an average yield by weight of 115 and two-sevenths bushels per acre: 30 acres of oats (sown on spring breaking) yielded 1,262 measured bushels, besides five large loads of oats which were fed in the sheaf. These oats tested 38 pounds per measured

bushel, making an average yield by weight of 49 and nine-tenths bushels per acre, of that part threshed. Thus the total yield, by weight, of wheat and oats on 112 acres, was 7,875 bushels.

I also had 5 acres of potatoes, which yielded, as near as I can estimate, 1,500 bushels. Also 20 acres of peas which made an enormous crop.

J. B. F. GEORGE.

Thus Mr. Georges' wheat and oats raised on 112 acres (or his crop exclusive of his potatoes and peas) at present prices, lack only $33 of equaling the value of the whole 160 acres at $20 an acre.

HARVEST SCENE ON THE RANCH OF F. SYLVESTER & SONS

HARVEST SCENE ON THE RANCH OF F. SYLVESTER & SONS

HARVEST SCENE ON THE RANCH OF F. SYLVESTER & SONS

AFFIDAVIT OF F. SYLVESTER & SONS

Monte Vista, Colo., Dec. 21, '91.

We hereby certify that the three views preceding are from photographs of the crop on our farm. We purchased this farm, 480 acres (a part of Cottage D. Farm), of the Colorado Valley Land Company, in the fall of 1890, paying therefor $20 an acre. The land was fenced and broken and had a small house and stable. We seeded 250 acres in wheat, 160 acres in oats, 15 acres in barley and 6 acres in potatoes. We have threshed only a small part of the wheat, and can therefore only estimate the yield. But judging from the yield of our neighbors' wheat, threshed, and comparing our crop with theirs, we should not hesitate to say that our wheat will average 50 bushels per acre. We have threshed only 20 acres of oats; we measured the ground, it yielded 100 measured bushels per acre. These oats test 45 pounds per measured bushel, making the yield by weight, 140 bushels per acre. The 20 acres threshed was probably a little better than the average of the whole crop, but we believe

---

It is safe to say that the crop of F. Sylvester & Sons, raised on the above mentioned land, will more than pay for the land and all the expense of raising the crop.

the whole 160 acres of oats will average 125 bushels per acre, by weight.

The barley threshed out 1,117 bushels by measure, and overran 1 pound to the bushel, making an average yield per acre of 76 bushels. We moved here from Ogden, Iowa, in March, 1891, and this has been our first experience in farming by irrigation. One man could have irrigated our whole crop after the lateral ditches were built.

F. Sylvester & Sons.

LA CARITA FARM BUILDINGS

LA GARITA FARM

This farm contains 2,000 acres, all under a high state of cultivation. It is one of the finest combined grain and stock farms in the Valley.

MEADOW FARM BUILDINGS

MEADOW FARM

This beautiful farm contains 6,000 acres of very fine hay and grass land; it is purely a stock farm.

NORTH FARM BUILDINGS

NORTH FARM BUILDINGS

NORTH FARM

The two foregoing cuts are from photographs of the North Farm buildings. This farm comprises 7,640 acres. It is a splendid grain and stock farm.

The buildings on the South Farm are nearly duplicates of those of the North Farm.

All of the above farms of the Colorado Valley Land Company are for sale. They will be sold entire, or will be cut up in tracts to suit purchasers.

The terms of sale are exceedingly liberal. On improved land a cash payment of *one-fourth*, and on unimproved of *one-tenth* is all that is asked; the remainder in six equal annual payments, six per cent interest.

For further particulars concerning the lands of the above companies, address

JAS. A. KELLY & CO.,
General Agents, Monte Vista, Colo.

BIRD'S-EYE VIEW OF DEL NORTE

DEL NORTE

Is the county seat of Rio Grande County, Colorado, and the oldest town in what is known as the San Juan country. The town-site was surveyed in 1872, though the town company was formed in 1871. At the present time Del Norte has a population of about 1,000 souls. The town is reached via the Denver and Rio Grande from Denver or Pueblo—distance from Denver 280 miles; altitude, 7,400 feet. The town is so situated as to be upon the line between the agricultural and mining sections. To the north and east of the town are the rich and rapidly settling agricultural and pastoral lands of the San Luis Valley; to the south and west are the great mines of San Juan. Del Norte is beautifully situated in a basin at the foot of the mountains, sheltered from the blasts of winter, and having the most delightful weather in summer. The Rio Grande River flows through the edge of the Del Norte townsite, and offers to manufacturing interests the finest water power in the world. Del Norte has some excellent business and dwelling houses, a fine public schoo building, three good church buildings above the average, the Presbyterian College of the Southwest (a staunch educational institution), a fine flouring mill of the latest roller process, two banks, a court house costing $30,000, a weekly newspaper, the *San Juan Prospector*, the United States Land Office, where all business regarding lands in this district must be transacted.

Del Norte has properly been called the "Gateway to the San Juan," being so situated as to control the entrance to the valley of the Rio Grande River, which leads directly to the heart of the San Juan mining country. The route up the Rio Grande will, undoubtedly, eventually form the main line to the San Juan country, having advantages of distance, grade, etc., possessed by no other route.

FIRST NATIONAL BANK OF DEL NORTE

Del Norte's position is such as to command trade from the mining, agricultural and pastoral sections of the Southwest, and must eventually become a place of great importance. The town of Del Norte is situated on mesa or table land, has all the advantages of good schools and churches, excellent climate, fine water for domestic use—no better anywhere—and is, withal, an ideal residence and educational center. Del Norte's especial pride is her schools and college. On Lookout Mountain, 600 feet above the town, is mounted a large telescope to be used in connection with the Presbyterian College of the Southwest. The view from the Lookout observatory is grand in the extreme. The streets of Del Norte are wide, and the town is noted for its growth of trees—mostly cottonwoods. Water for irrigating purposes is supplied by means of a main canal from the Rio Grande River, with laterals over the town-site along the sides of streets.

The distances from Del Norte to the following points are:

To Alamosa . . . . 30 miles.
To Saguache . . . . 35 miles.
To Villa Grove . . . . . 45 miles.
To Monte Vista . . . . . 15 miles.
To Veteran . . . . 18 miles.
To Summitville . . . . . 27 miles.
To Wagon Wheel Gap . . 30 miles.
To Shaw's Springs . . . 6 miles.
To Carnero . . . . 25 miles.
To Creede . . . . 40 miles.
To Lake City . . . . . . 85 miles.

Del Norte being the oldest town in the Valley has necessarily been compelled to stand the hardest sort of competition, but to-day is a live, wide-awake town, and holds a position that must command the attention of railroad builders, capitalists and home-seekers.

As a summer resort, Del Norte, the San Luis Valley and surrounding country have few equals. The days are cool and pleasant, while the nights are such

THE DEL NORTE FLOURING MILL.

as to render several blankets necessary for comfort at all seasons of the year. To the west of Del Norte thirty miles are the Wagon Wheel Gap Hot Springs, reached during the summer season by daily trains on the Denver and Rio Grande Railroad. The volume of travel to Wagon Wheel during the summer season is increasing every year, and it will not be many years before Wagon Wheel Gap will be one of the most noted health and pleasure resorts in the West.

North of Del Norte six miles, via a fine wagon road, are the Shaw Magnetic Hot Springs. The waters of these springs have wrought many marvelous cures.

The lakes and hills near Del Norte abound in game of all kinds. There are plenty of duck, geese, etc., in the lakes, while in the hills may be found bear, deer, elk, grouse, etc. The Rio Grande River is the finest trout stream in the West, and is visited during the summer season by hundreds of tourists and pleasure-seekers from all over the country. There are good hotels along the river for the accommodation of sportsmen and invalids. It is now getting to be quite the fashion to construct summer cottages along the Rio Grande, and the moneyed men of the South and East recognize the Upper Rio Grande country as the pleasantest place in the West to spend the heated term.

There is every reason for supposing that the demand for San Luis produce will more than equal the supply. The valley is situated in the midst of heavy mountain ranges. These mountains are full of precious metals, and the development of the surrounding mineral country will naturally call for heavy shipments of produce from the Valley. Nature appears to have done her best in providing here a valley capable of raising unlimited quantities of produce, and surrounding the Valley with a territory rich in minerals, the mining of which will naturally absorb

INTERIOR VIEW OF E. F. RICHARDSON'S LAW OFFICE

HOTEL RICHARDSON, DEL NORTE

the entire product of the valley. Here we have a country complete in itself—a great agricultural section and a perpetual home market.

The principal mines of Rio Grande County are at Summitville, twenty-seven miles southwest of Del Norte. There are several stamp mills at Summitville, a single gold brick from one of which was landed at Del Norte, and was worth $33,000, being the result of a 28-days' run. There is a good wagon road from Del Norte to Summitville. Senator Thomas M. Bowen, of Colorado, is a prominent operator in this camp, with his headquarters at Del Norte.

The new mines of Creede, forty miles west of Del Norte, are just now causing great excitement in mining circles, and have drawn much of their supplies from Del Norte. Creede has all the symptoms of a live mining camp, from which Del Norte is certain to reap much benefit.

The mines of interior San Juan are all tributary to Del Norte, which may yet become a point for treatment of ores. In addition to the above are the mines of Platoro, Conejos County, naturally tributary to Del Norte, which town also draws much support from the Carnero mines in Saguache County, twenty-five miles away. The town is one of the gems of the valley—wide-awake, enterprising, thrifty—and is worthy of the attention of the new-comer, as well as the confidence of the old-timer.

FIRST NATIONAL BANK.—The First National Bank of Del Norte occupies one of the most elegant banking quarters in the entire West. It was built expressly for them and is a model among the many banking houses of the United States. The First National is the outcome of the legitimate wants of the merchants of this city and ranchmen of the Valley for banking facilities, and has ever been conducted upon a conservative yet enter-

INTERIOR VIEW OF THE EWING HARDWARE CO.'S STORE

prising basis. The bank was organized May 6, 1890, with a capital of $50,000, and to-day has an additional surplus and undivided profits amounting to $3,000. The officers are: W. H. Cochran, President; J. J. Crosswy, Vice-President; C. W. Thomas, Cashier (and by the way he is the youngest bank cashier in the United States), and R. H. Sayre, Assistant Cashier. The directors are among the leading business men of Del Norte and the San Luis Valley.

THE DEL NORTE FLOURING MILL AND POWER COMPANY.—In sketching the different business houses whose enterprises have added materially to the growth and prosperity of Del Norte, we know of none more deserving of extended mention than the one under consideration. The Del Norte Flouring Mill and Power Company was organized this spring with Mr. Charles W. Thomas as Manager. They use the full roller process, and manufacture Pride of Del Norte, Valley Queen, Miners' Delight, Beatty's Burro and Cream of the San Luis Valley flour, the latter a fancy patent. They are also extensive dealers in graham, feed, etc. The mill is operated by the finest water power in the State of Colorado, and has a capacity of seventy-five barrels per day. The grain from which their product is made is grown in the San Luis Valley, and the product itself, owing to its superior excellence, finds a ready sale in all parts of the State. The manager of the mill is a courteous, honorable gentleman with whom it is a pleasure to transact business.

HOTEL RICHARDSON.—The first thing the traveling public want to know when they reach a town is where they can secure suitable accommodations, and will naturally turn to a work of this character for the desired information, so we feel it is a pleasure to give a brief mention of the Hotel Richardson. This house is most centrally located, and is the only

BANK OF DEL NORTE

first-class house in Del Norte. It is well supplied with light and airy rooms. These commodious apartments are furnished with a view to the comfort of the guests, and can be had either single or en suite. The first floor of this hotel is devoted to the dining-room, office and bar and billiard room. The menu will always be found to contain all the delicacies of the market, and of the choicest description. The bar and billiard-room is handsomely appointed, and is supplied with handsome fixtures which are in perfect taste and harmony, and is presided over by a mixologist who thoroughly understands his business. The manager of this very popular hostelry is Mr. E. R. Mosher, who has been in charge of the house about one year and has lived in the city four years, and has during that time won a host of warm friends. He is a courteous, well informed gentleman who has throughout his busy career ever sustained an untarnished reputation for honorable, fair dealing and sterling good qualities.

E. F. RICHARDSON.—No man in the entire San Luis Valley bears a better reputation, both morally and financially, than the gentleman whose name heads this sketch. He has been a resident of the city of Del Norte since 1885, and has in that time built up the leading and most lucrative practice in the city and in this portion of the valley. He has brought to his profession of attorney-at-law natural ability and attainments of a high order, and being a close student and a keen observer of men and methods, has naturally forged to the front in his chosen profession. Mr. Richardson occupies splendidly fitted up rooms in the Richardson Block, the largest building in the city, which he recently sold to Eastern parties. He possesses large real estate interests, all of the most substantial character. That he is devoted to Del Norte goes without saying, else he would

INTERIOR VIEW OF THE WEISS-CHAPMAN DRUG CO.'S STORE

not have invested so much capital in the city. Mr. Richardson's position of eminence has been attained by ever devoting his time and talents to the interests of his clients. He is a man who would scorn to adopt any of the unscrupulous methods of obtaining money so common with some attorneys.

THE EWING HARDWARE COMPANY occupies a more conspicuous place in the line of general and heavy hardware, wagons, implements, etc., than any other house in this section of the State. This enviable position has been gained by the honorable and intelligent efforts put forth by the members of the firm, who are intimately identified with the industries of the Valley, and who have figured

J. B. HOCKER, JR.
Sheriff of Rio Grande County

THE A. F. MIDDAUGH MERCANTILE CO.'S STORE

prominently in the growth and prosperity of Del Norte and the San Luis Valley. The facilities of this house meet the requirements in every particular, and are all that could be expected from a modern American institution of this character. The Ewing Hardware Company has been in business in this Valley thirteen years, having been established in 1878 and incor-

OLANDO BONNER
Treasurer of Rio Grande County

porated in 1884, and carry an extensive stock of everything usually found in establishments in their line, among which may be mentioned hardware, cutlery, iron, steel, nails, wire, powder, fuse, stoves, agricultural implements, etc. They are the pioneers in their line, and have a large and constantly increasing trade, due to their honorable and conscientious business methods.

JOHN CLEGHORN.—Mr. John Cleghorn, proprietor of the Columbia Avenue Livery Stables, first came to Del Norte in 1875. His stables are provided with all the modern conveniences, while in the matter of equipment there can be found a complement of fine buggies and carriages, elegant driving horses, as well as gaited saddle animals, and all patronizing this establishment will find in attendance polite and attentive drivers, grooms, etc. Mr. Cleghorn is a courteous, genial gentleman, honorable and fair in all his transactions. He is constantly purchasing the latest styles in buggies, thus keeping up with the times, and any person who contemplates taking a ride will cater to his own pleasure by first calling

M. B. GIBBS' MEAT MARKET

at this stable and taking a look at his supply of animals and vehicles, which are the best that money and experience can purchase. As demonstrating the esteem in which Mr. Cleghorn is held in private life, it is only necessary to say that he was Register of the United States Land Office six years, was Sheriff of Rio Grande County four years, and Mayor of Del Norte four years. He has lived in this city since 1875, with the exception of four years in San Juan County. Mr. Cleghorn is a representative citizen, and always takes a hand in every project for the advancement of his city, Rio Grande County and the San Luis Valley.

W. H. COCHRAN.—In the year 1875 Mr. W. H. Cochran removed to Colorado,

STORE OF GEORGE BEERE
Dealer in Ranch Produce, Fruits, Vegetables, Cigars, Confectionery, etc.

J. B. HAFFEY
Clerk of District Court, Rio Grande County

where he became interested in the newspaper business, first owning an interest in the Colorado Springs *Mountaineer*, and afterwards *The San Juan Prospector*, of Del Norte, with which he was connected for about ten years. During the time Mr. Cochran was in the newspaper business at Del Norte he held the office of Postmaster for seven years. In 1886

GEORGE A. SCIBIRD
Editor The San Juan Prospector

ran organized the First National Bank of Del Norte, of which he is President; and also organized the Del Norte Flouring Mills and Power Company, having as its object the utilization of the water power of the Rio Grande River. At the present time, Mr. Cochran is one of the Directors of the Public Schools of Del Norte, is a Trustee of the Presbyterian College of the Southwest at Del Norte, and a Regent of the State University at Boulder.

JOHN B. HOCKER, JR.—In the person of John B. Hocker, Jr., Rio Grande County has one of the most trustworthy and efficient officials in the State. The gentleman is a Sheriff of whom any county would have every reason to be proud.

Mr. Cochran was elected Treasurer of Rio Grande County, on the Republican ticket, and was re-elected in 1888. In 1884, after selling their interest in the *Prospector*, Mr. Cochran and his brother, John M. Cochran, engaged in the live stock business, and have succeeded in getting together a large lot of cattle, horses and land. In 1890 W. H. Coch-

LEE KAYSER'S GENERAL MERCHANDISE STORE

He has brought to the office that strict integrity and honesty of purpose so essential in the ideal officer of the law. He is a Democrat, and was elected to the position he occupies by a very handsome majority in a Republican county. He has been in office two years, and has lived in the Valley fourteen years, conducting a livery business in Monte Vista.

As a business man, Mr. Hocker has no superior. He is a gentleman of courteous demeanor, honorable and fair in all his transactions, and is widely and favorably known throughout the Valley as a representative business man, an honest, conservative and well-qualified officer, and an intelligent, progressive and liberal minded citizen.

ALFRED R. LUFTH'S SADDLERY AND HARNESS STORE

GEORGE C. BERLIN
Attorney-at-Law

OLANDO BONNER.—Chief among Rio Grande County's most estimable citizens is the gentleman whose name heads this article. Mr. Bonner is a Republican, and one of the very best in the entire San Luis Valley. He came here some eight years ago, and at once assumed a prominent position among the leading and yet conservative business men of this

ALDEN BASSETT
Dealer in Real Estate

always be counted on to do his share toward advancing the material interests of the San Luis Valley in general and Rio Grande County in particular.

J. B. HAFFEY.—A man who stands exceptionally high in the estimation of the citizens of Rio Grande County, is the subject of this sketch—Mr. J. B. Haffey, who has been a resident of the Valley for twenty years. His popularity, honesty and trustworthiness are amply proven by the fact that he has held the position of Clerk of the District Court for eight years, an honor few men attain in his age of continual change in office. Mr. Haffey has a reputation for honesty, probity and excellent business judgment unexcelled in the Valley and is one of

section of the State. He has held the office of Treasurer for two years, and has conducted the affairs of the position to which he was elected in a manner which has met with the heartiest approval of all concerned. Mr. Bonner is a gentleman of splendid executive ability and fine business qualifications. He is an admirable and trustworthy citizen, and can

JOHN POOLE'S DRUG STORE

its most responsible citizens. There has never been a time in the county's history when there was a legitimate movement on foot for its material advancement that Mr. Haffey was not interested in it, and he will always be found in the front rank, with his shoulder to the wheel, when Rio Grande County is to be benefited, either directly or indirectly.

L. D. MERCER.—Mr. L. D. Mercer has been in business here eight years, and has lived in the San Luis Valley off and on for nineteen years. Mr. Mercer, as a business man, is a typical "rustler," and with his indomitable pluck, energy and perseverance bids fair to become the Nestor of commercial circles. He occupies a neat and attractive store-room and

OTTO LEWIS'S BAKERY

C. W. THOMAS
Cashier First National Bank

carries a full line of clothing in every style. His line of gents' notions, neckwear, etc., is not easily duplicated, and during the existence of the house, strict integrity, sober business principles and a liberal spirit, has made a reputation and trade that is bound to increase each year of its wise management. There is also in connection a splendid assortment of

E. R. MOSHER
Manager of Hotel Richardson

desirous of pushing Del Norte and the San Luis Valley to the front as one of the commercial centers of Colorado.

THE A. F. MIDDAUGH MERCANTILE COMPANY.—The handsomely and elegantly fitted up store of The A. F. Middaugh Mercantile Company is most admirably arranged and conveniently situated, being one of the finest establishments of the kind in the entire San Luis Valley. The stock carried is a large and varied one and embraces a splendid assortment of dry goods, clothing, hats, caps, boots, shoes, groceries, produce, etc., in fact, everything usually carried in a first-class general merchandise store. Here will be found all of the correct styles and patterns and all the standard jewelry of all kinds, styles and prices, also dry goods, hosiery and ladies' furnishing goods. The clerical employes of the house are attentive, competent and desirous of pleasing, and those who patronize Mr. Mercer are assured of every attention, which means more than words, "come again." Mr. Mercer is always in the front rank of those who are

HENRY KIEL'S BLOCK

shapes—and all of the very best material. The house was established as it now stands some three years ago; Mr. A. F. Middaugh is President, J. E. Hasbrouck, Vice-President and Manager, and E. W. Pfeiffer, Secretary and Treasurer. The president of the company has been a resident of the Valley over fifteen years.

M. B. GIBBS.—Mr. Gibbs is a dealer in all kinds of fresh, salt and smoked meats. He does his own slaughtering and consumes monthly a large number of beeves, sheep and hogs. The business premises are clean, neat and commodious, and fitted up with all modern conveniences for the handling of his large trade. Mr. Gibbs is a thoroughly practical butcher, and since his inception in business here has met with the most flattering encouragement. He is a wide-awake, enterprising business man, and richly deserves the success he is certain to achieve. Mr. Gibbs is one of the old timers in this Valley, having first located here seventeen years ago. He is held in the highest esteem both in commercial and social circles for his many sterling

LEVI B. WILSON
Proprietor New York Cash Store

SHAW'S MAGNETIC SPRINGS

qualities, and is always to be relied upon to do his share towards advancing the material interests of the San Luis Valley and the city of Del Norte.

GEORGE BEERE.—Mr. Beere has lived in the San Luis Valley sixteen years, and has been in his present business a little more than one year. There can be found in his store a very fine selection of fresh fruits and ranch produce, in addition to which he carries an extensive stock of both foreign and domestic cigars, tobacco, candies, nuts and confectionery. His stock of cigars includes the most popular brands, and his supply of fruits is always fresh and wholesome. Mr. Beere also sells goods on commission, and his large and constantly growing trade is due to the fact that he is a man of perfect trustworthiness.

LEE KAYSER.—Mr. Lee Kayser has lived in the town of Del Norte twelve years. He has conducted his present business since 1887, succeeding H. Schiffer & Bro., who were the first parties to go into business in this city. Mr. Kayser's business premises are admirably fitted for the use to which they are put, presenting a neat and attractive appearance so essential to success in a line of business where the necessaries of life in the matter of food are supplied. Mr. Kayser carries one of the largest stocks of goods in the Valley, comprising groceries and provisions, dry goods, boots, shoes, hats, caps, underwear, gloves, furnishing goods, carpets, rugs and oil cloths, canned and dried fruits, salt meats, flour, grain, feed and everything to be found in a complete line of general merchandise. Mr. Kayser has ever maintained one of the representative establishments of the San Luis Valley, with whose material interests he has long been identified.

ALFRED R. LUFTH.—An enterprising and reliable institution engaged in the harness and saddlery line of business is

JOHN CLEGHORN'S RANCH

the establishment of Alfred R. Lufth, who bought the business of Mr. H. J. Burghardt about two months ago, although Mr. Lufth had been with the former proprietor about a year and in the business nine years. The trade of this house to-day is large and permanent, and is constantly increasing at a most satisfactory rate. The proprietor of this establishment is a gentleman who is thoroughly conversant with his business, and is held in high esteem by the community for his sterling business methods and many social qualities.

GEORGE C. BERLIN.—The gentleman whose name heads this sketch has been a resident of the San Luis Valley since 1883, but did not establish his present business until two years later. He is an attorney of the highest attainments and an unblemished character. He will practice in all Courts of the State, and has been more than ordinarily successful. Mr. Berlin has established a magnificent reputation for honorable treatment of friend and foe, and can always be depended upon to devote his entire time and all the talents of which he is possessed to the interests of his client. He is a keen, energetic business man, and has never been accused of adopting any of the unscrupulous methods of making money so popular among a certain class of attorneys. Real property, law and titles to real estate are made specialties. Mr. Berlin, hitherto as a member of the firm of T. A. Good & Co., also makes a specialty of Rio Grande County abstracts, and has every imaginable facility for transacting business in that line in a thorough and competent manner. The abstracts furnished can always be depended upon for accuracy and genuineness. Real estate and loans are also part of the business, and receive due attention. Although established only four years ago in the abstract business, Mr. Berlin has already achieved an envi-

FRED RABER'S RANCH

able reputation for thoroughness and reliability in this line. All business entrusted to him will receive personal attention and his most painstaking efforts.

JOHN POOLE.—One of the largest and most popular drug houses in the entire San Luis Valley is the house of John Poole in Del Norte, where is carried in stock all of the different kinds of drugs and chemicals, inclusive of all the proprietary and patent medicines of note. Mr. Poole has a graduate of pharmacy, Mr. John M. Shaffer, to attend the prescription department, and the public can rely upon having their prescriptions filled in the most accurate manner. Mr. Poole is also an extensive dealer in paints and oils, wall paper, books and stationery. He makes a specialty of fine fishing tackle. He has been in this business since 1885, was a county commissioner three years, and has resided in this Valley and in the town of Del Norte eighteen years, therefore he is one of our pioneers and one of Rio Grande County's most popular citizens.

NEW YORK CASH STORE.—The New York Cash Store is owned by Mr. Levi B. Wilson, who established the business one year ago last January. The business premises used are well arranged and admirably adapted for the business for which it is used. The New York Cash Store carries in stock a fine line of ladies' and gents' furnishings and fancy goods, dry goods, clothing and boots and shoes, of the latest and most fashionable kinds. Also notions, toilet requisites and a list of mercantile articles that our space is too limited to enumerate. This house, by virtue of the strict basis of honorable dealing on which it is conducted, has secured a large and lucrative patronage. Mr. Wilson has lived in this valley six years, and in the State ten years. His reputation for honesty, conservatism, courteousness and square and upright dealing is second to none. Mr. Wilson

C. A. ELLIOTT'S RANCH

was not educated as a merchant, but as a member of the ministry. He devoted his former life in Ohio and Kansas to this profession, but on account of throat troubles came to Colorado and adopted a mercantile pursuit.

ALDEN BASSETT.—In the great tidal wave of progress and substantial improvement that has continually applied its operative forces to the great ship of commerce, it is quite positive that no single line of business, or those engaged therein, has contributed more energy and propelling power to this continual and unprecedented prosperity than those men of ability and enterprise who are known in the commercial world as real estate dealers, and in this numerous list we find none more deserving of extended reference than Mr. Alden Bassett, who established his present business on the first of September of the present year. Mr. Bassett has been a resident of the Valley since 1873. He occupied the position of County Clerk for eleven years. He has accurate and intimate acquaintance with Del Norte and San Luis Valley real estate, both as to its present and prospective values. He is thoroughly identified with the interests that affect the Valley and the town of Del Norte. He is also a Notary Public and Conveyancer, and is a gentleman of known and tried energy.

OTTO LEWIS.—In a complete review of the business interests of this city, the establishment of Otto Lewis—Del Norte Bakery—is entitled to prominent mention. The business was established eleven years ago, and has been in its present location nine years, and owing to Mr. Lewis' practical knowledge of the requirements of the people, has gained a steady and gratifying increase of trade. He deals in staple and fancy groceries, cigars, tobacco, etc., and carries a large and choice selection of those articles. Mr. Lewis bakes all kinds of bread,

J. G. BAUER'S RANCH

cakes, pies, etc. The articles of food manufactured in this establishment are noted for their excellence and purity, none but the best brands of flour and other ingredients being used. Mr. Lewis stands high in mercantile circles as a man of probity and honorable business methods.

BANK OF DEL NORTE—The banks of Del Norte have long held a name and reputation throughout the banking world for reliability and excellent business judgment. Their enterprising and yet conservative management has been a most important factor in the development of her natural resources. Their growth and usefulness has been in keeping with the progress of Del Norte's commerce, and they constitute the bedrock upon which is founded the city's future prosperity. One of the most prominent fiscal institutions in the West is the Bank of Del Norte, of which Mr. Asa F. Middaugh is proprietor and E. W. Pfeiffer Assistant Cashier. It was established ten years ago, and from the day of its inception until the present has been looked upon as one of the leading banking houses in this part of the State. The officers of the bank have always been prominently identified with the material interests of Del Norte and the San Luis Valley, and the bank itself has always been regarded as one offering the safest and most absolute security to depositors. Its reputation among the financial institutions of the West is second to none.

GEORGE A. SCIBIRD, editor and business manager of the *San Juan Prospector*, at Del Norte, was born at Bloomington, McLean County, Illinois, February 12, 1856, and resided there until 1873. He attended the public schools of Bloomington until he was fourteen years of age, at which time he was placed in his father's printing office, the *Leader*, as an apprentice at "the art preservative." Mastering the mechanical part of the business,

ROBERT CORSON'S RANCH

Mr. Scibird went to Colorado at the age of seventeen years, and has been identified with the papers of Colorado Springs, Fairplay, Leadville and Del Norte since that time. Coming to Del Norte in 1876, he accepted a position on the *Prospector*, which he held almost steadily until April, 1884, when he purchased a half interest in the office, which he holds at this time.

Whatever of success Mr. Scibird has attained may be credited to his own individual effort. He is in comfortable financial circumstances, has a good home at Del Norte, and is at the head of a successful country paper which does not owe a dollar and has held the field against all comers. As an editor, the efforts of Mr. Scibird looking toward the development of the San Luis Valley and Southwestern Colorado have been almost unlimited. The *Prospector* is recognized as one of the leading and most successful papers of the San Luis Valley.

HENRY KIEL.—Among the strictly first-class liquor houses in this city is that conducted by the above named gentleman, whose establishment dates back some eighteen years. Mr. Kiel is one of the oldest and best known settlers in the San Luis Valley, and his house certainly deserves a prominent place in a work of this nature. Inasmuch as his house is conducted on the strictest principles of honesty and integrity, it has gained a well-merited reputation as a reliable house. A specialty is made of handling the better grades of wines, liquors and cigars. Mr. Kiel is one of those affable gentlemen who make friends with all with whom he comes in contact, and that he is successful is attested by the large number of people who visit his establishment. In this connection, it may be mentioned that Mr. Kiel is also dealer in the purest and best ice that is procurable in this portion of Colorado. He is a representative, wide-awake and

CHAS. FAIRCHILD'S RANCH

progressive business man, and has legions of friends.

SHAW'S MAGNETIC SPRINGS.—From Del Norte a ride of five and one-half miles, over a delightful road, brings you to Shaw's Magnetic Springs, esteemed by the people of the San Luis Valley as one of its chief attractions. That the claim is well founded cannot be denied by any one who has visited this pleasant resort and bathed in its welcome waters. The proprietor informed us, on our first visit, that his baths were free to anyone who had ever found a better, but that up to date no free bath had ever been claimed under the proposition. The baths are, indeed, delightful, and nicely arranged for the pleasure and comfort of guests. The main building, of which we show a cut, is a substantial stone structure. The cottages are frame, nicely and pleasantly fitted up. The surrounding scenery is picturesque in the extreme. The State Park, adjoining the grounds, is a tract of about 6,000 acres which, on account of its magnificent natural scenery, was donated by the Government to the State for the purpose of a State Park. Added to these facts, the fine trout fishing in the La Garita, the Rio Grande Canals and Lake, and the Rio Grande River, all within a convenient distance of the Springs, make them one of the most delightful resorts in Colorado for recreation and pleasure. But with all the advantages of Shaw's Springs as a resort, the proprietor makes still greater claims for them as a sanitarium. An analysis of the water shows sulphur, soda, magnesia and iron in nearly equal parts, making a happy medical combination that works upon the blood, kidneys and stomach, making a pleasant and complete specific for all chronic diseases arising from a derangement of those organs. It is claimed for these waters that they have never failed to cure rheumatism, sciatica, kidney complaint, catarrh, dyspepsia, or

EDWIN J. SHAW'S RANCH

any kind of blood poisoning. For terms for board, baths, teams, fishing and hunting outfits, address the proprietor. Certificates of cures effected by these waters will be furnished on application. For substantial corroboration of the merits claimed for these Springs, you are referred to Hon. Judge Blodgett, United States Circuit Court Judge, Chicago, Ill.; Hon. Thomas M. Bowen, Del Norte, Colorado; Dr. Samuel Rapp, 352 East Fiftieth street, New York City. Address all correspondence to John H. Shaw, the proprietor, Del Norte, Colorado.

FRED RABER.—This gentleman has 380 acres in wheat, oats, potatoes, peas and hay. He has resided here for four years and is considered as one of Rio Grande County's most enterprising farmers.

C. A. ELLIOTT.—In a work of this character, the ranch of which Mr. C. A. Elliott is the owner, deserves special mention, which we gladly give it. This ranch is second to none in this Valley. It is well watered, has splendid buildings and fences, and every improvement that is usually found on the property of an enterprising, progressive ranchman, including the best kinds of labor-saving machinery, good stock, etc. Mr. Elliott's crops can always be counted upon as being splendid, for he devotes his attention to his ranch, and makes it a point never to be behind his neighbors. He is a courteous, pleasant gentleman.

JOHN GEORGE BAUER.—The Bauer ranch is located four miles from Del Norte. It consists of 320 acres mostly in wheat, also is handled here about 200 head of stock. Mr. Bauer is a worker and develops his farm to the highest state of cultivation.

ROBERT CORSON.—The gentleman whose name heads this sketch has earned the well merited reputation of being one of the most progressive and prosperous ranchmen in the Valley. This reputation

L. D. MERCER'S RANCH, NEAR DEL NORTE

he has earned by devoting his attention to farming on a scientific basis, studying the soil and the climate, and exercising good judgment and proper care. His ranch, known as the Crag ranch, from the large number of crags adjoining it, is, for these reasons, one of the most productive in Rio Grande County, and is a model for others. So far as improvements are concerned, Mr. Corson is in no sense behind his neighbors, possessing, as he does, every requisite for successful ranching. He is an urbane, obliging gentleman, who has a host of friends.

CHARLES FAIRCHILD.—The editor of "San Luis Valley Illustrated" takes much pleasure in writing this sketch of Mr. Charles Fairchild's ranch, which is, without the least doubt, one of the best in the State of Colorado. Mr. Fairchild is an old settler in this part of the country, and owns a ranch of which any man might well be proud. It is well watered and the improvements are of the most substantial kind. He raises splendid crops of all kinds. Mr. Fairchild is also an old miner, and owns several promising mines in the Creede district, of which he was one of the earliest prospectors. His property is considered by experts to be among the best in the neighborhood, and will doubtless prove very valuable in due time.

EDWIN J. SHAW.—Among Rio Grande County's most prosperous and progressive ranchmen is the gentleman whose name appears at the head of this short article. Mr. Shaw's ranch is one of the handsomest in the Valley, and is stocked with the best class of animals. His houses are not only neat, but they are most substantial. The ranch has an abundance of water, and the soil, which is naturally fertile, yields magnificent crops of all kinds of cereals under Mr. Shaw's skillful and energetic tillage. Of him it may truthfully be said that he is one of the most enterprising ranchmen in the San Luis Valley.

L. MONTOYA.—The gentleman whose

GEORGE R. MALLETT'S RANCH

name heads this sketch is one of the oldest settlers in the San Luis Valley, and unlike a majority of his countrymen —being a Mexican—he believes in farming on an extensive scale. His ranch is not only large, but what is more to his credit, it is well cultivated, and his improvements rank with the best in the Valley. Mr. Montoya is a progressive, public-spirited citizen, who is fully up to the times in the use of labor-saving machinery and the better class of stock. He is far in advance of his race in many things, and particularly in the matter of ranching, owning, as he does, one of the best ranches in the Valley, on which he invariably raises splendid crops.

GEORGE R. MALLETT.—Few ranchmen in the San Luis Valley have a better piece of ground than George R. Mallett, and still fewer raise larger or better crops or have neater buildings. Mr. Mallett is a practical man, as is evidenced by the crops he markets. He farms his land as it should be farmed, giving it his personal attention and best efforts, and never neglecting any point that may add to the fertility of the soil or the quality of the crops. He uses the best of machinery and stock, and raises crops second to none in the Valley, quality and quantity considered. Mr. Mallett is a successful, enterprising man in every sense of the word.

H. J. SCHRADER.—The above named gentleman has resided here since 1873. He has 160 acres in hay and potatoes, also raising and making a specialty of small fruits. He is one of the most successful ranchmen in the San Luis Valley.

H. J. SCHRADER'S RANCH

WAGON WHEEL GAP

Wagon Wheel Gap is widely known on account of the curative powers of the springs at that point. It received its name from some wheels being found in the Gap by one of the early freighters, which were probably left there by General Fremont when he went through. At the springs, which are about a mile from the Denver and Rio Grande Railroad, and at the Gap itself, is conducted a hotel by N. Patten & Son. They have resided here for nine years, and as the great crowds at the hotel in the summer attest, they are popular and affable hotel men.

L. MONTOYA'S RANCH

HOW TO REACH THE SAN LUIS VALLEY

FROM THE EAST

The Denver and Rio Grande Railroad is the only line running through the San Luis Valley. After the traveler has arrived at either Denver or Pueblo, he will take a seat in one of the Rio Grande's magnificent cars and ride to Salida. If the traveler is in a narrow guage car, no change will be necessary at that point, but one must change at Salida from the standard to the narrow gauge train, which leaves Salida in the morning and traverses the entire Valley. First of the Valley towns to be reached is Villa Grove, then follow Moffat, Garrison, Mosca and Alamosa. At the last named place the road branches off in two directions. On the Durango branch are the towns of La Jara, Conejos and Antonito, and on the Del Norte branch are Monte Vista, Del Norte, Wagon Wheel Gap and Creede.

On the line of the Denver and Rio Grande Railroad in the Valley will be found the following points of scencic interest:

MOUNT SIERRA BLANCA.

This magnificent mountain, 14,469 feet high, is remarkable for being the highest mountain in the Rockies. It presents a very imposing appearance, as it stands right out from the plains. It is at the eastern entrance to the San Luis Valley, which is itself on an elevation of 7,000 feet, so that Sierra Blanca stands straight up from the Valley a sheer uplift of about 7,500 feet. The mountain is very massive, and stands out like a mighty promontory at the point where the Veta Pass separates the northern half of the Sangre de Christo range from what is known as the Culebra range extending down into New Mexico. Its appearance is most remarkable and pleasing in effect. Grand as Pike's Peak appears from the Ute Pass, it cannot be seen anywhere to such advantage as Sierra Blanca for a hundred miles across San Luis Valley.

Immense forests of pine and hemlock occupy the lower slopes of the mountain, but timber all ceases by the time one-third of the height is reached. Three gray granite peaks crown the summit, and between these, down in the deep gorges, eternal snows and icy glaciers reign supreme. The road which runs around the base of the mountain, coming from the north to Fort Garland, describes the arc of a semicircle for over thirty miles; this will give some little idea of its size.

THE SANGRE DE CHRISTO RANGE.

"Where the Pass of the Veta divides the long chain,
And Mount Blanca's proud summit o'ershad-
ows the plain,
San Luis expands; where each object is rife
With a thousand details from the dramas of life!
Then turret and cupola crowd on the eye,
And fortress and temple seem traced on the sky!
The mountains their bulwark — their mirror
they make
The clear running brooklet or the deep placid
lake!
Say, stranger, what clime of the South hast
thou seen
So meet for a poet—a painter—a queen!"

This magnificent range of mountains is often seen in travels among the Rockies. Extending in a semicircle from Salida to Santa Fe, they form, with the Colorado range, which extends from Long's Peak to Pike's Peak, what is known as the Front range of the Rockies; and the only break between these two of any moment is the valley of the Arkansas. And yet, after you have crossed this range, notwithstanding that it contains the highest peak of the Rockies in Sierra Blanca, you have not yet touched the Main range, or what is known as the Continental Divide. The Main or Snowy range of the Rockies begins in the northern boundary of Colorado, in the Medicine Bow Mountains; and as it approaches the center of the State, breaks up into several branches. It is only by observing the course of the rivers that the watershed or backbone of the continent can be traced. Now the Front Range only separates the waters of the Rio Grande from those which flow into the Mississippi; as the waters of the Mississippi flow into the Gulf of Mexico, and the waters of the Rio Grande do the same, this range, therefore, does not divide the continent. We must find, then, a range that throws the waters down the western slope into the Gulf of California. The Saguache range does this, for down the western slope of this range flow the waters of the Grand, the Green and the Gunnison, all of which flow into the Colorado, which river, after running its wondrous course through unrivaled canons, finds its way into the Gulf of California. As we shall see when we come around the other half of the circle and cross the Saguache range by Marshall Pass, that range divides near Salida and runs in two directions; the one southwesterly to form the Main range, and the other southeasterly to form the Sangre de Christo chain, and the broad San Luis Valley, through which the Rio Grande flows, separates them.

But even this is not all of the Rocky Mountains by any means. There are miles and miles of mountains west of both the Saguache and the Sangre de Christo ranges. Altogether, what is known as the Rocky Mountain system embraces an area of close upon a million square miles. How insignificant the Alps, in territorial extent, in comparison with the Rockies! In height there is but little difference. As for scenery, there is such a succession of lofty peaks, magnificent ranges, lovely parks and vales, majestic rivers, castellated rocks, grand and sublime canons, wondrous cascades, waterfalls, natural fountains and mammoth boiling springs, that even Switzerland cannot equal, much less excel, the Rockies in any single point above mentioned.

SAN LUIS VALLEY.

"Here silence reigns,
And naught there is to mock
The far-off murmur of the mountain rill,
As if a voice in solemn accents breathed
O'er the wide expanse and lone park 'Be still!'"

This is one of the four great parks

that separate the main range of the Rockies from the front range. These parks stretch through the entire State of Colorado, beginning on the borders of Wyoming, and extending down into New Mexico. They are known as North Park, Middle Park, South Park and San Luis Park. San Luis Park, or Valley, runs from the point where the Sangre de Christo range diverges from the Saguache just south of Salida, to Santa Fe in New Mexico; and from Fort Garland, opposite Sierra Blanca, to Del Norte. It is 210 miles long and 100 miles wide, and contains more acres than the whole State of Connecticut. It has once been a great inland sea 10,000 square miles in area; even now there is a sort of beach at the foot of the mountains which resembles that of the ocean. It is entirely surrounded by lofty mountains, some of which exceed 14,000 feet in altitude. The park itself is on an elevation of 6,500 feet, so that from the plain the surrounding mountains stand straight up for nearly 8,000 feet, and they are snow-clad everywhere.

The atmosphere is strikingly transparent, due to the dryness of the air and entire absence of fogs. This enables one, in crossing the park, to see the distant mountains most vividly all around. They can be distinguished quite easily at the distance of a hundred miles, when, to all appearance, they seem to be not more than twenty miles away. Although traveling on a fast train, Sierra Blanca is never out of sight whenever we wish to look at it, for at least four hours. No less than seventeen distant peaks, lofty and snow-clad, can be counted from one spot, while innumerable smaller mountains everywhere encircle the plains. The principal peaks, besides Sierra Blanca, are Trinchera and Culebra on the east, and on the west, from the Toltec Gorge northward, Conejos and other lofty summits of the Sierra Mimbres range. In the east, the mountains rise very abruptly from the park; on the west not so much so, as they fall back, one tier above another, until all are mingled together in one conglomerate mass. The park is watered by thirty mountain streams, nineteen of which flow into San Luis Lake, an extensive body of water in the upper portion of the Valley; the rest enter the Rio Grande del Norte, a river which has its source in the perpetual snows of the San Juan Mountains, and flows through the center of the park from Del Norte to Espanola in New Mexico. San Luis Lake is several miles in length and has no outlet. It is surrounded by what is called a savannah of luxuriant grass saturated with the waters which flow into it from the melted snows of the mountains.

The finest farms, or ranches, lie along the northern rim of the park at the foot of the mountains. More than 500,000 sheep and many thousand head of cattle and horses live out on the open plains the year round, and find all the pasture they need. Irrigation is resorted to for agricultural purposes and artesian wells are numerous. A number of ranches are worked and owned by Mexicans; and with them the most primitive methods of cultivation are in vogue, as much so as ever they were in the time of Abraham. Some American and English farmers have adopted more modern methods, and they are certain to become prosperous and even wealthy.

The Rio Grande Railroad traverses San Luis Park in a zigzag way. It runs due west for twenty-four miles from Fort Garland to Alamosa, then due south for twenty-nine miles to Antonito, then west again for thirty miles to the Toltec Gorge. The first and only inhabitants of this park were the nomadic Indian tribes, who found all the fish and game they wanted in the streams and meadows and in the mountain fastnesses around the park. Then came the gold hunters of Coronado's time, who hunted for the precious metal with more than an Indian's instinct and energy. These were followed by the hardy explorers who became the pioneers of those who now occupy the many mining camps. Following these came the Mexican herdsmen and shepherds, who had nobody but the Indian to dispute their right to the rich pasture lands. All except the latter class have given way, and these are fast doing so, to the more enterprising American farmer or ambitious foreigner, who together are fast turning this solitary wilderness into a beautiful garden where the vegetables, fruits and cereals have superseded the pampas grass, and where the Colorado cattle and Merino sheep are taking the place of the Indian mustang and the Mexican steer.

Persons who desire further information relative to the San Luis Valley should address S. K. Hooper, General Passenger and Ticket Agent Denver and Rio Grande Railroad, Denver, Colorado; or F. A. Wadleigh, Assistant General Passenger Agent Denver and Rio Grande Railroad, Denver, Colorado.

THE PUBLISHER